MIRAGE OF THE NORTH SEA

By: Mustafa Nejem

PROLOGUE

"Mirage of the North Sea" is a story that unfolds in a fictional world surrounded by a strange and mysterious North Sea. The main character dreams of traveling to the North Sea and exploring its secrets. After a mysterious turn of events, they embark on a challenging journey in search of the secret of the North Sea and discover supernatural powers residing beneath its waves.

CONTENT

CHAPTER 1
THE DISCOVERY

Liam was a resident of Eldoria, a charming coastal town known for its peaceful and smooth-running affairs. Inhabitants of the town carried out their everyday activities with a sense of serenity that had been a defining characteristic of life in Eldoria for countless generations. Life in Eldoria had a leisurely pace, a rhythm that appealed to the majority of the population. However, for Liam, this serene routine of village life failed to satisfy his craving for excitement and adventure.

From a very early age, Liam's imagination had been captivated by the mysteries of the North Sea, a colossal body of water that enveloped his coastal hometown. To Liam, the North Sea was not merely a stretch of ocean; it represented a boundless realm brimming with untold stories, legends, and puzzles waiting to be unraveled. For him, this vast expanse of water signified far more than a mere geographical feature; it was an entire universe teeming with uncharted possibilities and concealed secrets.

Each night, he would dream of embarking on adventures across uncharted waters, encountering magical creatures, delving into submerged cities, and uncovering hidden treasures concealed beneath the sea's depths. This yearning for exploration had become an integral part of his very being.

Liam worked with his dad in the fabric business that had been in the family for generations.

While Liam held a deep affection for his family and cherished his bonds within the close-knit village

community, he couldn't shake the persistent yearning for something more expansive and profound. As he toiled day in and day out, weaving cloth and peddling it at the nearby marketplace, a sense of weariness and tedium began to set in. The repetitive rhythm of his daily life, although reliable and comforting for many, couldn't quell the burning curiosity that drew his thoughts persistently toward the North Sea.

The allure of journeying into the enigmatic depths of this vast ocean stirred within him a profound excitement and longing for exploration that couldn't be extinguished. The prospect of embarking on adventures into the uncharted waters was something that continued to dance in his mind, a tantalizing call to a world beyond the horizon.

On an ordinary day, as Liam roamed through the shelves of Eldoria's library, where ancient and somewhat dusty tomes lined the oakwood shelves, he stumbled upon an extraordinary revelation that was destined to alter the course of his existence.

Tucked away in an obscure nook of the library, obscured by layers of accumulated dust and possessing frayed, time-worn edges, he encountered an ancient scroll. With a measured and delicate touch, he unfurled it, revealing a map so intricate and detailed that it appeared to breathe with the very essence of the North Sea.

The heart of the map bore an unmistakable mark, a point of unparalleled intrigue. It was precisely in the center of the sea, boldly emblazoned as if to declare its significance to any intrepid soul who would lay eyes upon it. This singular point was no ordinary location; it was a cryptic place that had garnered the status of legend among mariners and scholars alike. It was none other than the "Tear of the Abyss," a name whispered in awe and reverence by those who knew of the tales surrounding this enigmatic treasure trove hidden within the depths of the North Sea .

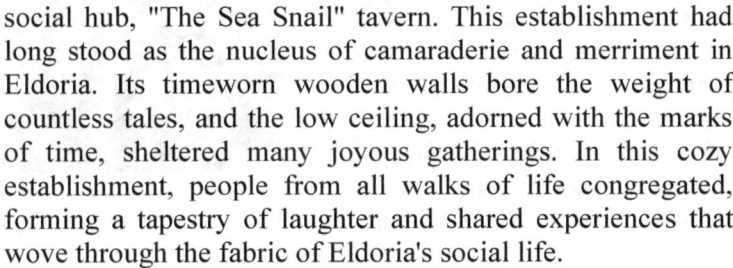

The Tear of the Abyss wasn't just a shining gem; It was a story that had been passed down from generation to generation. Legend had it that whoever managed to find it, would gain magical abilities and the ability to solve the deepest riddles of the North Sea.

To Liam, that map was like a sign, the opportunity he'd been waiting for all his life. His eyes sparkled with excitement as he carefully studied every detail of the map.

Without a moment to spare, Liam swiftly departed from the library, his heart brimming with anticipation, and made his way to the heart of the village's

social hub, "The Sea Snail" tavern. This establishment had long stood as the nucleus of camaraderie and merriment in Eldoria. Its timeworn wooden walls bore the weight of countless tales, and the low ceiling, adorned with the marks of time, sheltered many joyous gatherings. In this cozy establishment, people from all walks of life congregated, forming a tapestry of laughter and shared experiences that wove through the fabric of Eldoria's social life.

For Liam, "The Sea Snail" represented more than just a place of revelry; it was an ideal haven to unveil the treasure he had discovered.

His companions and confidants, with whom he had shared countless stories and dreams, awaited within, and he was eager to regale them with the newfound secret of the "Tear of the Abyss."

Upon arriving at the tavern, Liam met two of his best friends: Mark, a tall and physically strong man, who was very fearless and this pushed him to face the unknown and accept any challenge that came his way. And Emma, a very beautiful and intelligent woman. In the group, she was known as the no-nonsense voice, always concerned about the safety and well-being of her friends.

With the scroll in hand, Liam walked to a sort of makeshift dais in a corner of the tavern. In that corner, the innkeeper used to entertain customers. Without wasting any time, he shared his exciting find with the local audience, explained the authenticity of the map and the existence of the Tear of the Abyss.

Told them about the amazing stories about the North Sea, the magical creatures that were said to inhabit its waters, and the lost treasures that lay in its depths.

Mark, always willing to seek new adventures, didn't need much to make his decision, he agreed to join the search for the Tear of the Abyss, he wanted to explore the mysterious waters of the sea and face extreme challenges.

On the other hand, Emma, while sharing the excitement, had her reservations, mentioning the dangers that lurked in the North Sea: the sudden storms that could appear, the dangerous sea creatures, and the treacherous eddies of the deep. Despite her concerns, Emma understood Liam's excitement and pledged her support in this quest. For years, they had shared adventures and secrets, and I wasn't going to leave him alone on this new journey.

The next day, Liam set sail for the coast, where his small boat was moored, ready to set sail in search of the Tear of the Abyss. As he loaded provisions onto the ship, a name crossed his mind: Sarah.

He had heard of a local sailor, a young woman who knew the waters of the North Sea like the back of her hand. If anyone could safely guide them through the treacherous waters, that person was Sarah.

After doing some research in the harbor and asking questions of the local sailors, Liam managed to locate Sarah. She was a woman with dark hair and bright eyes. Sarah had spent most of her life at sea, sailing through the changing waters of the North Sea.

The trio was complete, but Liam had a card up his sleeve. During his childhood, he had witnessed the magical powers of an elderly hermit named Ethan, who lived on the outskirts of town.

Ethan was known for his wisdom and extraordinary magical abilities. Although he used to lead a solitary life, Liam knew that his magical knowledge could be essential on the journey.

Liam and his friends returned to the coast to look for Ethan. They found him in his cabin hidden in the woods, surrounded by scrolls, books, and magical objects. Liam explained his quest and the purpose of his adventure. Ethan, though initially reluctant, recognized the twinkle in Liam's eye and agreed to join the group. He knew that his magical knowledge could be essential on the journey and that his role in the quest could be crucial.

Together, Liam, Sarah, Mark, Emma, and Ethan prepared to set sail for the uncharted waters of the North Sea. With the ancient scroll in hand and the promise of a legendary treasure, his adventure was just beginning.

They were filled with excitement as they embarked on a journey that would lead them to face challenges, uncover secrets, and change the course of their lives forever.

The search for the Tear of the Abyss had begun. The future was full of promise and danger, and Liam and his friends were determined to bravely explore the unknown. Their journey was just beginning, but they were ready to face what the North Sea had in store for them.

CHAPTER 2
MARINE RUMORS

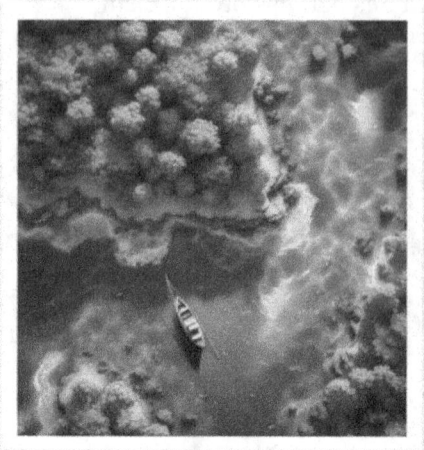

The North Sea stretched out before them mysteriously, like a blank canvas waiting to be filled with discoveries, on board, conversations were lively, and everyone shared their expectations and desires for the voyage.

While Sarah steered the helm with skill and experience, Mark and Emma took care of the sails and ropes, making sure everything was in order on the boat. Liam stared at the horizon, deep in thought about what they might find in their search for the Tear of the Abyss. Ethan, the group's magic expert, retreated to a quiet corner of the ship and began flipping through one of their old magic books, looking for clues that might help them on their journey.

During their journey, as they ventured further, these explorers couldn't help but become privy to the enchanting tapestry of legends that clung to the North Sea's expanse.

These were no mere stories but cherished heirlooms, tales whispered in hushed tones from parents to children, generation after generation. Among the murmurs of Eldoria's sailors, seasoned by the ocean's salt and trade winds, there lay accounts of awe-inspiring encounters with colossal sea beasts,

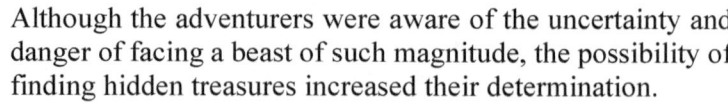

whispered rumors of islands that appeared and vanished mysteriously, and the hallowed narratives of long-lost treasures, resting on the seabed's timeless embrace. The allure of these sagas further fueled their determination to embark on a journey of exploration and discovery.

The stories heightened the excitement and anxiety of Liam and his team.

One of the rumors told of a giant creature known as the "Guardian of the Deep." This castle-sized sea beast was said to patrol the waters of the North Sea, protecting the most valuable treasures that lurked in its depths. The tales varied in detail, but they all spoke of the vastness of this creature and how ferocious it could be.

Although the adventurers were aware of the uncertainty and danger of facing a beast of such magnitude, the possibility of finding hidden treasures increased their determination.

Another rumor spoke of an enigmatic island, hidden in the middle of the sea, that housed an ancient temple. In that temple, it was said, magical artifacts of unimaginable power were kept. The brave ones who had tried to reach the island had never returned, which only stoked the curiosity of Liam and his team.

The prospect of finding lost treasures and discovering magical artifacts drove them forward, despite warnings from locals about the island and its mysterious temple.

The crew stayed up all night, with guards on the ship to keep an eye out for potential dangers. The darkness of the North Sea added an aura of mystery to the voyage, and the silence of the ocean was only interrupted by the gentle creak of the boat as it glided over the waves.

As the clock ticked down and the moon rose in the sky, team members reflected on the challenges they were willing to face.

At dawn, Liam approached Sarah, who was still handling the helm deftly. He stopped beside her and, looking at the horizon, decided to break the silence of the morning with his questions. "Sarah, what do you think of all this? Of the rumors and the treasures we might find. Do you really think it's possible?"

Sarah, staring at the horizon, replied calmly. "Liam, the North Sea is a place full of secrets and surprises. Rumors sometimes have some truth to them, but they can also be somewhat exaggerated. The important thing is that we are here, together, ready to discover what awaits us. The adventure is not only in the destination, but also in the journey itself. I'm excited for everything we'll explore together."

Sarah's words lifted Liam's spirits even more, filling him with hope. He looked at his team members, each with their own expectations and motivations for embarking on this journey. They knew that the North Sea was a place full of dangers and mysteries, but also of promises and treasures. They were willing to face whatever it takes to reach their goal.

Ethan, the hermit who possessed magical abilities, decided to join the conversation.

For most of the journey, he had remained silent, immersed in his thoughts and his books. Now, he turned his gaze to the group with a twinkle of excitement in his eyes.

"We should not underestimate the power of the North Sea. Legends speak of lost treasures, but also of unimaginable challenges. We must be prepared for the unknown and trust in our abilities," he said. As the day progressed, team members continued to share stories from their own lives and experiences.

Their gatherings were characterized by hearty laughter, interspersed with moments of deep contemplation and a palpable anticipation of the future. Each member of their fellowship brought their unique motivation for venturing into the unknown, yet there was a collective enthusiasm that bound them together – the desire to uncover the hidden mysteries concealed within the Tear of the Abyss. They were united by a resolute spirit to confront any obstacles, surmount any hurdles, and uncover the truth that lay shrouded in the enigmatic tales of the North Sea. Their shared dreams served as the compass guiding them through the uncharted waters that awaited them.

The North Sea continued to stretch out before them, full of secrets and surprises.

As they moved into the unknown, the excitement and anxiety of adventure mingled in their hearts. As the ship gently rocked in the waves, Liam looked up at the horizon, thinking about the rumors they'd heard and the challenges they'd face in their quest for the Tear of the Abyss.

They knew that the road ahead would be full of dangers and discoveries, but they were willing to face it.

The team of adventurers realized that their journey was just beginning. The North Sea had so much more to offer, and they were determined to explore the unknown, discover lost treasures, and write their own story in the mysterious waters of the ocean, they continued their journey, ready to face whatever the North Sea had in store for them.

CHAPTER 3
INITIAL JOURNEY

The first few days of sailing are uneventful, and the crew adapts to life at sea with ease. Sarah, with her experience as a navigator, deftly handles the rudder, expertly keeping the boat on course. Mark and Emma, with their strength and skill, take care of the sails and ropes, making sure everything is in place and working properly. Liam, who leads the expedition, scans the horizon deeply thoughtfully, while Ethan, the hermit with magical abilities, is reclining in a corner, consulting his old books for clues that might help in the search.

As night descends upon the vast expanse of the North Sea, the crew finds themselves in a state of readiness, mentally and physically, to confront the trials that lie ahead during their oceanic passage. The shroud of darkness casts an enigmatic veil over their voyage, imbuing it with an essence of mystique.

Amid this nocturnal ambiance, the sea itself seems to hold its breath in a profound silence, save for the intermittent murmur of the boat's timbers as it gracefully traverses the undulating waves. As the journey continues, the crew remains vigilant, their senses heightened, fully cognizant of the necessity to remain alert, knowing that potential perils may lurk in the obscurity of the night.

The passage of time stretches into elongated hours that slowly transition into days, and as they progress, an ominous tempest materializes on the horizon, its dark clouds and turbulent winds signaling a formidable challenge ahead. The crew, cognizant of the impending tempest's fury, takes on a coordinated effort to confront the turbulent maelstrom as a

unified front. They adhere to a vigilant watch rotation, each member assuming their turn to remain awake and attuned, recognizing the collective responsibility they bear in sustaining the vessel's buoyancy and ensuring the safety of all aboard.

In this precarious journey, each individual serves as a crucial component within the interwoven network that safeguards the ship from the tempest's relentless onslaught.

At long last, after enduring a seemingly interminable period of tempestuous turmoil, the menacing storm commences its gradual descent into serenity. The thick, oppressive clouds begin to scatter, unveiling a tranquil expanse of blue skies that stretches infinitely above. The once-volatile waters, which had surged and roiled with unbridled ferocity, gradually acquiesce

to the calming influence of nature. A collective sense of relief washes over the ship as the crew gazes aftward, their expressions a mixture of exhaustion and contentment. In their hearts, they find satisfaction and pride, knowing they have triumphed over the inaugural and formidable trial of their grand expedition.

The experience of weathering the storm has further strengthened the team's bonds. They have shown their courage in the midst of adversity, they know that the North Sea will not be an easy place to conquer. Each of them is aware that teamwork is essential to face the challenges that await them.

As they progress on their journey, the crew is eager to explore and discover new challenges. After a few days, they come across mysterious islands emerging out of nowhere, with white-sand beaches and lush forests. These islands are a reminder of the beauty and diversity of the marine world, but also of the mystery that surrounds these time-forgotten lands.

On one of the islands, they find the ruins of an ancient city, its buildings covered with vegetation and its streets invaded by nature. Adventurers explore the ruins, searching for clues to the Tear of the Abyss. Although they can't find definitive answers, the beauty and mystery of the ruins fill them with awe. It's as if they're walking in a place that time had forgotten, full of secrets and wonders.

As they go, they encounter other vessels, some of whom share stories of their own adventures in the North Sea.

As they traverse their watery path, they are regaled with tales of yore, stories that speak of fortunes buried beneath the ocean's depths, thrilling meetings with denizens of the deep, and tests of seafaring acumen that would confound even the most seasoned mariners. Each narrative is like a gust of wind stoking the flames of their anticipation and fortitude to press forward in their relentless pursuit of the fabled Tear of the Abyss. Every anecdote serves as an enduring reminder that the North Sea is a realm teeming with enigmas and escapades, each

one ready to be unveiled and embraced by those daring enough to explore its secrets.

The team also realizes that the North Sea is a place full of amazing marine life.

They spot playful dolphins leaping alongside the boat, majestic whales emerging from the depths, and schools of brightly colored fish swimming around them. The beauty and diversity of marine life are breathtaking. It's like they're sailing in a magical world filled with amazing creatures. Each sighting fills Liam and his team with awe, reminding them of the wonder and magic of the North Sea. The team gathers on deck to enjoy the serenity of the sunset. As they watch the sky turn warm, they know their journey has just begun.

The North Sea has offered them a taste of their unpredictable nature, but they are ready to explore the unknown and discover the secrets of the ocean that stretches out before them. They are filled with determination and excitement as they prepare for the adventures that lie ahead in their search for the Tear of the Abyss.

They know the journey will be challenging, but also full of amazing discoveries.

CHAPTER 4
MEETING THE SIRENS

Suddenly, emerging from the waters in a majestic arc, they saw a group of amazing creatures: mermaids. Mermaids were magical beings of the sea, known in stories for their incomparable beauty and ability to bewitch sailors with their sweet songs. They approached the ship with unmatched grace, their long hair flowing in the water, and their eyes shining with a mysterious light that hypnotized all who looked at them. They were half-woman, half-fish creatures, with tails of shiny scales that sparkled in the light of the setting sun. Their voices were melodious and magical, and seemed to fill the air with a dreamy feeling.

Liam's crew found themselves in a state of utter awe as the sirens approached the ship. They had heard of these creatures in sea legends,but had never imagined encountering them in the flesh. Mark, the most fearless member of the team, stared with wide eyes and a smile of amazement on his face.

Emma, always the no-nonsense voice of the group, was captivated by the beauty of the mermaids, but she also maintained a caution in her gaze.

Liam, at the center of this magical scene, was overwhelmed with excitement and disbelief. Mermaids had been part of his dreams since he was a child, and here they were, real and in front of him. He knew that this encounter could be an unexpected twist in his search for the Tear of the Abyss.

As the mermaids, Their enchanting smiles illuminating their visages, commenced their melodious songs. Their voices carried the essence of the natural world, a harmonious

symphony drawn from the very soul of the seas. Their music wafted through the air, enveloping the crew in a tender embrace of serenity. Each musical note felt like an ancient narrative, recounting the age-old enigmas and marvels of the North Sea, unveiling tales of the denizens dwelling within its watery realm, and hinting at the treasures concealed beneath the cerulean depths.

As the magical chords of mermaids filled the ship, the crew found themselves trapped in a dreamlike state. Almost without realizing it, they began to move to the rhythm of the music, their feet marking an invisible beat on the ship's deck. The melody of the mermaids made them feel a deep connection with the sea and its secrets.

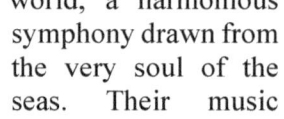

Liam, Mark, Emma, and the rest of their comrades found themselves utterly captivated by the entrancing melodies. Their expressions revealed a complex medley of emotions—joy, wonder, and a hint of wistfulness. The mermaids had transported them to a realm where legends intermingled with actualities, where aspirations materialized into reality.

The sirens' song continued, and although they knew they should be wary of these magical creatures, they couldn't help but feel a deep connection with them. They were witnessing something exceptional, something that only a lucky few got to experience.

The encounter with the mermaids would mark an unforgettable chapter in his journey to the Tear of the Abyss, a page full of magic, beauty and mystery.

The crew stood mesmerized, gazing in wonder at these

enchanting beings, creatures whose existence had been the stuff of legends and folklore throughout their lives. This was a truly exceptional meeting, a rare privilege granted to only a fortunate handful. They all understood that mermaids held the keys to age-old sea secrets, and they were on the brink of unveiling some of those long-held mysteries.

One of the mermaids, who introduced herself as Marina, spoke in a melodious voice that seemed to caress the air. "Welcome, brave North Sea travelers. We have heard of your search for the Tear of the Abyss and wish to provide you with valuable information that will guide you on your path. However, as is customary among our people, we require a favor in return."

The crew paid close attention, realizing that the sirens' assistance could be extremely helpful in their quest for the Tear of the Abyss. As the leader, Liam spoke for the team, expressing their willingness to go to great lengths to obtain information about the Tear of the Abyss. "We are prepared to undertake any task necessary to gain knowledge about the Tear of the Abyss. Please, share with us the favor you seek," he said.

Marina smiled as she shared her request. "Our request is simple, but it is not without its dangers. Beyond these waters, on a remote island, lies a magical plant that is essential to our survival. We call this plant the 'Flower of the Sea', and it is one of a kind. This

flower grows only on that island and is a vital source of magical energy for us mermaids.

However, that island is fraught with danger and inhabited by ferocious creatures that protect it. We need you to bring it back so we can share it with you."

The crew responded with understanding and determination, agreeing to carry out the task as requested by the sirens. Marina then proceeded to offer them specific and detailed information regarding the location of the island, including how to recognize the rare Sea Flower they sought. She also emphasized the potential challenges and dangers they might encounter during their journey, such as hostile sea creatures and natural traps on the island. The crew expressed their

gratitude for the valuable guidance provided by the mermaids and, with unwavering resolve, began making preparations for their voyage to the distant island.

With the echo of the sirens' song still ringing in their ears, they turned away from those mystical creatures and ventured out into the vast North Sea, in search of the mysterious island.

The mission they had been given was undoubtedly dangerous, but they also understood that it was a unique opportunity to gain valuable information about the Tear of the Abyss.

When they finally arrived on the island, they were met with stunning scenery.

The island was a true botanical wonderland, with its vibrant and abundant plant life. The crew found themselves immersed in a lush, almost jungle-like environment that was vastly different from what they had encountered on their journey so far. Towering trees, their leaves glistening as if touched by magic, stretched toward the heavens, creating a mesmerizing canopy above. The forest floor was adorned with an array of colorful flowers, their hues so unique and exotic that the crew couldn't help but be captivated by this newfound beauty.

The quest for the Sea Flower proved to be quite challenging. Navigating through the thick, untamed forests of the island was no simple feat.

The crew encountered an array of peculiar and unknown creatures, all of which seemed to be guarding the mystical plant they sought. Mark and Emma, known for their agility and physical prowess, assumed the role of pathfinders, expertly hacking their way through the dense foliage and creating a path for the rest. Liam, Sarah, and Ethan remained vigilant, ever watchful for any potential dangers that might lurk in the shadows, ready to step in and shield their companions if the need arose. This was a true test of their teamwork and determination.

Following several grueling hours of exploration, they finally stumbled upon the very plant that the mermaids had spoken of. The Sea Flower exuded an enchanting, ethereal glow, and its fragrance was as sweet as the most delicious fruit. Their elation was palpable as they realized they had successfully located the elusive flora. With great care, they proceeded to collect it, understanding the vital importance of their mission.

Yet, their journey back to the ship would not unfold as smoothly as they had initially anticipated. Challenges and obstacles lay ahead, ready to put their skills and determination to the test.

As they approached the shore, a gigantic sea creature emerged from the waters, it was a sea beast of colossal proportions, with glowing scales and eyes that seemed to contain the wisdom of the seas, it blocked their path, its imposing presence inspiring fear in the crew. They knew that facing such a creature would be an almost impossible task, but they couldn't give up.

Ethan, with his knowledge in magic, decided to try to communicate with the gigantic sea creature in an effort to negotiate. He used an ancient and respectful language, full of reverence for the creature. To everyone's surprise, the creature responded in a friendly manner, seeming to understand the importance of the Sea Flower for both mermaids and the balance of the sea itself.

The conversation that followed was enigmatic and brimming with symbolism, but in the end, the creature allowed the team to return to the ship with the prized Sea Flower.

His kindness and wisdom left the team in awe, and reminded them that the sea was full of secrets and amazing creatures, some of which were willing to collaborate with the adventurers. The crew couldn't help but feel grateful for the creature's generosity, as it might as well have opted for a more adverse path.

Back on the ship, they were reunited with the mermaids, and Marina received the Sea Flower with gratitude. Keeping his promise, he shared valuable information with the team. He told them of a hidden island in the heart of the North Sea, a place where the entrance to the lair of the Tear of the Abyss was believed to lie. He also warned them about the challenges they would encounter in their search.

The crew was excited by the new information they had acquired. Despite the obstacles they knew they were willing to face the challenges that the North Sea had in store for them.

They knew that each step brought them one step closer to their goal of unlocking the mysteries of the Tear of the Abyss, and that filled them with determination.

CHAPTER 5
THE HUNT FOR THE PEARL OF THE ABYSS

The information provided by the sirens had led Liam's team to a dangerous new stage of their search in the mysterious North Sea. The Tear of the Abyss seemed to be at his fingertips, but there was still a long way to go and numerous challenges to overcome. Their next task: to find the mythical Pearl of the Abyss, a vital ingredient that would allow them access to the Lair of Tears.

The Pearl of the Abyss was considered the magical core of the Teardrop, a rare and powerful gemstone. Without it, the entrance to the Tear's lair remained sealed, and its location was kept secret for centuries. But now, with the guidance of the mermaids, Liam and his team embarked on the hunt for the Pearl.

The island they were to head to was even further east in the North Sea, a region known for its treacherous waters and unpredictable weather.

As they approached the island, dark clouds hovered over the horizon, a harbinger of the coming storm. They knew they must hurry and find the Pearl before the storm caught them in its fury.

The island, known as the Pearl Island, was a desolate and fog-shrouded place. The trees seemed to twist into strange shapes, as if the island itself were alive and whispering forgotten secrets. The atmosphere was charged with a mysterious, gloomy aura that made the crew's hair stand on end. The search for the Pearl of the Abyss would not be easy, and the island presented them with an unsettling

environment that challenged their nerves and bravery.

The quest to find the Pearl of the Abyss led them on a challenging journey through the heart of dense, untamed forests. With their innate survival skills, Mark and Emma, the team's formidable adventurers, took the lead. They used their expertise to navigate the intricate maze of trees, thick undergrowth, and wild terrain.

Ethan, the magical mastermind of the group, played a crucial role throughout the quest. His profound understanding of mystical arts and ancient spells proved invaluable. With his guidance, they overcame magical obstacles, deciphered ancient enchantments, and moved ever closer to their elusive goal. Each step they took brought them deeper into the mysterious heart of the forest, where secrets and dangers lurked around every corner.

With his innate magical abilities, Ethan took on the role of a mystical compass, detecting the subtle yet potent magical energies radiating from the Pearl of the Abyss. His extraordinary talents served as their guiding light as they navigated the island's challenging terrain. At his command, the very air seemed to whisper secrets, revealing the path that would lead them to their elusive prize.

As they drew nearer to their destination, the magical presence in the atmosphere intensified, creating a palpable aura of enchantment that enveloped them.

With each step, they felt the resonance of ancient and powerful magic growing stronger, confirming that they were indeed on the right path to uncover the Pearl of the Abyss.

However, the island would not hand over its treasure to them easily. In their search, they encountered unexpected obstacles. Hidden traps and mysterious creatures complicated their progress. The roots of the trees seemed to come to life, twisting and forming obstacles in their way. Strange birds with shining eyes watched them from the treetops, like guardians of the island. Each step forward was a challenge and a test of his determination.

As they made their way around the island, the weather took a turn for the worse, and the coming storm finally broke out.

The rain lashed the island and the wind howled around it. The crew continued their search, drenched and battling the force of nature.

Each step became more difficult, but they knew they couldn't afford a break. The rain soaked their clothes and the wind made their steps unsteady, but their determination drove them forward. They knew the Pearl of the Abyss was worth it, and they wouldn't let the storm stop them.

Finally, after days of tireless searching, Ethan felt a surge of magic stronger than ever. They knew they were near the Pearl of the Abyss. They followed her through a dense forest until they came to a clearing shrouded in fog. In the center of the clearing, on a stone pedestal, shone the Pearl, a magical treasure of unparalleled beauty.

Liam and his team approached cautiously, knowing that this was a pivotal moment in their quest, and that acquiring the Pearl brought them one step closer to their ultimate goal.

Carefully, Liam picked it up and put it in a special chest, making sure it was protected.

The Pearl of the Abyss radiated a soft, mysterious light, and they could feel its magical power filling the air

19

around them. They knew that they had made a significant breakthrough in their search for the Tear of the Abyss.

The Pearl of the Abyss was a jewel of astonishing brilliance and mystery. Its surface seemed to contain an entire universe of flashes of light that reflected the dreams of those who looked at it. It was a reminder of the magic and wonder the world still held for those willing to venture into the unknown. It was as if this jewel carried with it a fragment of the secrets of the North Sea, and its beauty took the breath away of those who had the privilege of beholding it. They guarded the Pearl carefully, knowing that its power was a key piece in their search for the Tear of the Abyss.

However, his victory was not complete. As they prepared to return to the ship, a mysterious creature emerged from the mist. He was a guardian of the island, a half-man, half-beast creature whose eyes shone with ancient wisdom. He seemed to be the protector of the Abyss Pearl and was unwilling to allow it to be taken away without a confrontation.

The battle that followed was intense and challenging. The creature was formidable and used its knowledge of the island to its advantage. Liam and his team fought bravely, using all their skills and working together to confront the Guardian. Mark and Emma, with their strength, came together in a coordinated attack. Sarah maneuvered skillfully in the fight, while Ethan used his magic to weaken the enemy.

The battle was a test of their determination and courage, and although it proved to be a difficult fight, in the end, they managed to defeat the guardian of the island.

The creature, wounded and defeated, disappeared into the mist, allowing Liam and his team to return to the ship with the Pearl of the Abyss. They were exhausted but triumphant, knowing that they had overcome a major obstacle in their search for the Tear of the Abyss.

Finally, after a grueling struggle, they managed to defeat the guardian and earn his respect. The guardian, wounded but still noble, told them about the importance of the Pearl of the Abyss and how its power was linked to the Tear of the Abyss.

With the Pearl of the Abyss in their possession, the crew returned to the ship and set sail from Pearl Island, leaving the storm and dangers behind.

A sense of triumph and relief filled the air as they walked away from the island and continued their journey towards the lair of the Tear of the Abyss.

The Pearl of the Abyss was a priceless treasure and a symbol of his perseverance. They knew they were closer than ever to solving the secrets of the North Sea and reaching the Tear of the Abyss. With the Pearl of the Abyss glowing in their possession, the team of adventurers faced a future full of promise.

CHAPTER **6**
THE OATH OF ALLEGIANCE

As they gazed at the gem in awe, they had a sense of solemnity filling the air. They knew they had to take an oath of loyalty, a shared commitment to their cause and their pursuit. The Pearl of the Abyss was not only a treasure; it represented their togetherness, their determination and their respect for the mystery of the North Sea.

Liam, with his determined gaze and firm voice, took the floor. "We have come far in our search for the Tear of the Abyss. We have faced dangers and challenges that tested our strength. But our journey is far from over. As we approach the lair of the Tear, we will be presented with even greater challenges and deeper secrets. It's time to take an oath of allegiance, a shared commitment toward our goal." Liam pressed on, his resolute voice reverberating through the forest glade.

"We make an unbreakable vow to stand by one another's side, to confront each hurdle with bravery and sagacity, and to persist unyieldingly in our quest for the Tear of the Abyss. Together, we are an unwavering team, and we will face whatever challenges lie ahead with unwavering resolve."

May this gem bear witness to our oath and guide us on our journey. Together, we are stronger, and together, we will uncover the secrets that the North Sea jealously guards."

The team nodded solemnly, joining Liam's oath with determination. Their hearts were filled with purpose and hope as they prepared to face the challenges that awaited them in their quest for the Tear of the Abyss.

Sarah, staring at her, nodded and said, "We hold in our hands the Pearl of the Abyss, the key that will allow us access to the lair.

But we must remember that it will not be an easy road. Magical creatures, traps, and unfathomable mysteries await us. We must stay strong and loyal to each other."

Mark and Emma, with their undeniable strength and bravery, joined in the oath. "We are here to protect each other, to fight together against any obstacle that stands in our way.

The Tear of the Abyss is our shared goal, and we are committed to achieving it, no matter what."

Ethan, with his knowledge of magic and his wisdom, spoke solemnly. "The North Sea is a magical and ancient place. As we move forward, we must remember that we are visitors into your world. We must respect their secrets and protect their balance."

As each crew member took their oath of allegiance, the connection between them strengthened. They knew the road ahead was fraught with challenges and dangers, but they would support each other and maintain their shared commitment.

The Pearl of the Abyss was not only a treasure, it was a symbol of their shared adventure and the wonders and mysteries of the North Sea.

The jewel shone with a magical light that seemed to contain the very essence of the sea.

It was a constant reminder of his commitment to this pursuit. The Pearl was a beacon of hope and a reminder that their goal was closer than ever.

The North Sea, with its beauty and mystery, remained an unexplored world, full of treasures and secrets waiting to be discovered. The Tear of the Abyss, with its promise of supernatural powers and ancient mysteries, was becoming a nearer and nearer target. The team of adventurers was ready to continue their journey, to explore the depths of the sea.

As the ship moved forward, the crew prepared for a new journey full of challenges and discoveries. They knew they were ready to face whatever the sea had in store for them, united in their cause and committed to their shared goal.

CHAPTER 7
THE SUNKEN CITY OF LYRIA

The crew sailed purposefully through the waters of the North Sea, following the magical glow that rose from the depths of the sea. The Pearl of the Abyss lay safely in their chest, and its glow lit up the deck of the ship, constantly reminding them of the importance of their quest. They were near the mysterious Sunken City of Lyria, a place of legend and mystery that was believed to contain vital clues about the Tear of the Abyss.

The city, according to ancient tales, lay at the bottom of the sea, hidden from the eyes of most people. Its former inhabitants were said to be keepers of marine secrets and had left clues as to the location of the Tear of the Abyss. The glow of the Pearl of the Abyss gave them hope that they were finally close to uncovering these mysteries hidden at the bottom of the sea.

As they approached the location marked by the brilliance, excitement and awe filled the crew. Lyria, a city that had been submerged in the depths of the sea for centuries, loomed before them like an enigma waiting to be deciphered. The city was known for its immense power and wealth, built deep in the sea and inhabited by magical creatures. However, over time, it had disappeared from the sight of navigators, becoming a legend that only a few believed.

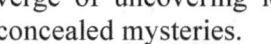

The city of Lyria appeared before them, rising from the depths of the sea. Its impressive towers and domes stood as a testament to the grandeur of the past. The crew couldn't help but be awestruck by the city's captivating beauty and the enigma it held. They were fully aware that they were on the verge of uncovering long-concealed mysteries.

The radiance of the Pearl of the Abyss had led them to this submerged city, instilling hope that they were on the verge of unraveling the mysteries surrounding the Tear of the Abyss.

Mark, with his keen eyesight, was the first to notice a flash in the water. He pointed excitedly to the horizon and exclaimed, "There, in the west! There is a glimmer of light in the depths of the sea."

The crew looked in Mark's direction and saw the flash, a magical glow rising from the seabed. They knew they were near Lyria, the place they had sought for so long.

The ship approached the glow, and soon they began to glimpse the outlines of the submerged city. The ancient structures rose from the bottom of the sea, covered in corals and seaweed.

23

Lyria stood before them, a place of mystery and wonder, where the answers to their questions might be hidden.

They were excited to explore this place full of history and secrets, ready to discover what awaited them in the ancient sunken city.

As the ship anchored near the sunken city, the crew prepared to explore Lyria. They donned their diving suits to move with ease in the depths of the sea, and equipped their magic lanterns to illuminate the dark underwater world. With the Pearl of the Abyss in their chest, they were ready to dive into the depths of Lyria. They were anxious and excited for the adventure that awaited them in this underwater city, hoping to find vital clues about the Tear of the Abyss. They were determined to explore every nook and cranny of Lyria

and uncover its hidden secrets. It was an important moment in their journey, and they were ready to dive into the mystery of the deep sea.

Upon their arrival in the city, they were greeted by the breathtaking beauty and magnificence of its structures. The streets and squares were embellished with age-old sculptures and intricate mosaics. The walls of the buildings were adorned with mystical inscriptions, adding to the air of wonder and enchantment that enveloped the city.

Despite being submerged for centuries, the city seemed to be in a surprising state of preservation.

The streets of the city were full of history and mystery. Ancient buildings towered majestically

around it, and the inscriptions on the walls seemed to contain hidden secrets. Every step they took in Lyria reminded them of the magnificence of this time-forgotten city and the secrets they might be about to discover in its depths.

Ethan, with his knowledge of magic, examined the inscriptions on the walls and the sculptures. "These inscriptions appear to contain important information," he announced.

"They talk about the Tear of the Abyss and his relationship with Lyria. It seems that the city had a crucial role in protecting the Tear."

As they explored the city, Ethan approached the inscriptions and sculptures to study them closely. His knowledge in magic allowed him to better understand the meaning behind these ancient symbols.

 Soon, he announced to the crew that the inscriptions spoke about the Tear of the Abyss and how Lyria had an important role in protecting it throughout history. The information they had been seeking for so long was closer than they had imagined.

As they explored further, they discovered a large square in the center of the city. In the center of the square, a statue of a magical creature with a pearl in its claws held a stone slab with a series of inscriptions.

Sarah walked over and began to read aloud, "The Tear of the Abyss lies at the heart of our world, a treasure and a mystery. Lyria was its guardian for centuries, but the city fell into oblivion."

As they continued to explore the submerged city, they found themselves in a large plaza at its center. In this square, they saw a statue of a magical creature holding a stone slab with inscriptions .

Sarah walked over to the slab and began to read aloud the words engraved on it. The inscriptions spoke of the Tear of the Abyss, mentioning that it was a treasure and a mystery that had been guarded by Lyria for many centuries, although over time the city fell into oblivion.

The crew realized that they had found vital clues about the Tear of the Abyss and its connection to Lyria.

The crew was fascinated by the revelation. Lyria had been the guardian of the Tear of the Abyss, a place of immense power and knowledge.

But over time, the city plunged into the depths of the sea, and its existence became a forgotten legend. Ethan continued to investigate the inscriptions and discovered a passage that spoke of a ritual necessary to access the Tear of the Abyss. "To get to the Tear, we must perform an ancient ritual at the Temple of Tides.

It seems that the temple is the key to solving the secrets of the Tear."

The crew realized that they had found valuable clues in Lyria. The city had been the guardian of the Tear of the Abyss, and the Temple of Tides was the key to unraveling its secrets. They knew they had to find the temple and perform the ritual if they wanted to get closer to their ultimate goal.

The team continued to explore Lyria, recording inscriptions and taking notes on the location of the Temple of Tides. The sunken city was a place of mystery and wonder.

CHAPTER 8
THE UNDERWATER PASSAGE

While exploring Lyria, Mark noticed a secret passage in one of the city walls. An ancient statue had been moved slightly, revealing an opening that led into the unknown. Intrigued, Mark walked over and examined the passage. "I think I've found something!" he exclaimed excitedly.

The crew gathered around the passage, with magic lanterns lighting the way. They didn't know where this passage led, but they were determined to follow it and uncover more secrets of the North Sea. The passage took them through a labyrinth of underwater tunnels, each decorated with magical inscriptions and ancient ornaments. It was evident that this path had been created by ancient inhabitants of Lyria, as if it was meant to take someone to a specific place.

As they went, the darkness and mystery of the passage enveloped them. Every step they took brought them closer to even more dangerous depths, but they were determined to keep going.

The glow of the Pearl of the Abyss in the chest was his guide in the darkness, his beacon of hope.

Finally, the passage led them into a vast and majestic underwater cavern. In the center of the cavern, lay an ancient stone altar covered in inscriptions and magical symbols. It seemed to be the heart of this underwater labyrinth.

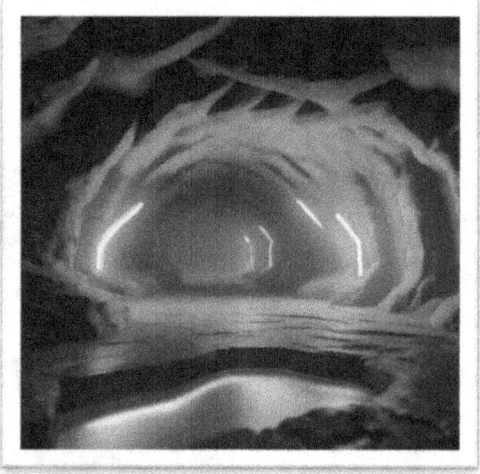

Ethan examined the inscriptions on the altar and announced, "This place is the Temple of Tides, mentioned in the inscriptions of Lyria. This is where we must perform the ritual to access the Tear of the Abyss."

The crew knew they had reached a crucial point in their search. The ritual they would perform in the Temple of Tides would bring them closer to the Tear of the Abyss, and perhaps finally reveal its secrets.

The ritual required each member of the crew to participate, combining their magic and energy with the Pearl of the Abyss.

They began the process, following the inscriptions and steps of the ancestral ritual.

As the ancient ritual continued, the underground chamber became aglow with a mesmerizing, magical light, casting an enchanting hue over everything. An aura of mystical energy swirled around, and the water surrounding them appeared to pulse with life, its magical currents dancing through the air. The crew experienced a profound sense of connection, not only with each other but also with the very essence of the sea.

Finally, the ritual reached its climax, and the Pearl of the Abyss began to glow brightly. A magical portal opened in the center of the altar, revealing an even deeper passage. They knew that this was the path to the Tear of the Abyss, the place they had sought for so long.

They entered the new passage, following the glow of the Pearl of the Abyss. But what awaited them in the depths was beyond their expectations.

The passage led them to an underwater world full of amazing and dangerous things.

They found themselves surrounded by giant corals that looked like trees underwater, brightly colored fish swimming around them, and magical creatures they had never seen before. It was a place full of beauty and wonder. However, there were also dangerous things. They found schools of giant jellyfish with venomous tentacles and water currents that were like underwater rivers, and could be swept away if they weren't careful. They were in a world of surprises and challenges, ready to explore and face whatever came next.

As they made their way through the passage, the crew realized that they were not alone in these depths. A deep, ominous murmur filled the water around him. They knew that something was lurking in the shadows, something ancient and powerful.

Out of the blue, a colossal silhouette ascended from the abyss, unveiling a mythical creature adorned with enormous, writhing tentacles and fierce, penetrating eyes.

This astonishing and fearsome sight was a revelation, a living legend that had seemingly sprung from the tales of folklore and mythology.

The sea creature approached the crew, its tentacles writhing in the water. He seemed to be guarding something, as if guarding the entrance to a sacred place. The crew realized that they had to face him if they wanted to move forward in their search for the Tear of the Abyss. The fight with the sea creature was a really big battle, where the crew used all their skills and magic to fight the monster. The bug's tentacles were very strong and dangerous, but the team was no slouch in their determination and bravery. The Pearl of the Abyss, shining very brightly, seemed to be supporting them in the fight.

After a very difficult fight, the creature finally retreated and swam deep into the sea. The crew had won the battle, but they knew their adventure wasn't over yet.

As they ventured further into the submerged tunnel, they descended to even greater depths, where an encompassing shroud of darkness and enigma enveloped their surroundings. The crew steeled themselves for the uncharted territory that lay ahead, fully aware that they were drawing nearer to the Tear of the Abyss. The Pearl of the Abyss had faithfully led them to this point, and their resolve to attain their ultimate objective remained unyielding.

As they made their way into the depths of the passage, they wondered what other challenges and secrets awaited them. The crew was united by their oath of allegiance, their determination, and their bravery. Together, they were willing to face any obstacle that stood in their way to the Tear of the Abyss and the mysteries that still remained to be discovered in the North Sea.

CHAPTER 9
UNEXPECTED ALLIES

After the intense battle with the Leviathan, the team took a well-deserved break. They sat around the Tear of the Abyss, which still shone on its stone pedestal, like a star at the bottom of the sea. They knew that this magical gem possessed ancient knowledge about the North Sea, its past, and its secrets. However, accessing this wisdom would not be so simple. To unravel the mysteries hidden in the Tear of the Abyss, they needed the collaboration of friendly sea creatures. The crew understood that the sea was full of amazing beings, some willing to help, and others, like the Leviathan, who were fierce and protective. Their next task would be to find these friendly beings and gain their trust to unlock the ancient knowledge they sought. They knew that this was the key to unlocking the deepest secrets of the North Sea and its role in the history of the world.

While the explorers gazed in astonishment at the Tear of the Abyss, they noticed a radiant, magical aura gently emanating from the gem. This luminous energy began to unfurl throughout the underwater cavern, creating an otherworldly display. It was as though the gem was transmitting a

message, a signal, to the mystical denizens of the deep sea, akin to a mystical summons that reverberated through the profound waters.

Suddenly, a group of friendly sea creatures emerged from the shadows. They were magical and majestic beings, each with unique characteristics that made them special. Among them were naiads with wavy hair, newts with fish tails, and mermaids with melodious voices that filled the space with their magical songs. These creatures were the guardians of the deep, ancient beings who had guarded the North Sea for countless centuries.

The sea creatures delicately surrounded the crew, showing their benevolence and acceptance.

They recognized humans as the current guardians of the Tear of the Abyss and were willing to share their knowledge and wisdom.

The merfolk engaged in a conversation using an age-old, underwater language that resonated through the sea. Simultaneously, the mermaids serenaded the explorers with enchanting songs, infusing the surrounding atmosphere with an enchanting and mystical ambiance. This interaction solidified a profound connection between these magical

beings and the human adventurers. It marked the initiation of an exchange of knowledge that would unveil the most profound enigmas concealed beneath the North Sea and shed light on its significance in the history of the world.

Ethan, thanks to his ability to understand ancient languages, was able to establish effective communication with the merfolk.

He approached them respectfully and asked them questions about the Tear of the Abyss and its role in protecting the North Sea.

Nerx, one of the merfolk, responded with a solemn tone, and his words reverberated through the water: "The Tear of the Abyss holds immense sacredness. Across countless generations, safeguarding it has been our solemn responsibility because it houses the profound wisdom of the sea. This luminous gem serves as a repository of the ocean's secrets and is the guardian of our history, connecting us to the ancient tales and knowledge of our underwater realm.

Its brilliance signifies the harmony and equilibrium of the North Sea, and it is an emblem of our connection with the vast aquatic world."

Their knowledge is essential to maintaining balance in these waters. We understand that they are interested in accessing their power, and we are willing to offer our assistance in this quest."

The conversation between Ethan and the merfolk unfolded with mutual respect and a shared understanding of the importance of the Tear of the Abyss in preserving the underwater world.

The human adventurers had gained the sympathy of these magical guardians of the sea, which would allow them to learn and access the ancient knowledge they so craved.

The naiads approached Sarah gracefully and handed her a necklace adorned with a twinkling golden shell. They explained to him that inside the shell was the magic needed to activate the Tear of the Abyss. Sarah accepted the necklace gratefully, understanding that this object would play an essential role in the next stage of her mission.

Meanwhile, the mermaids, with their mesmerizing melodies, began to share crucial information about the ritual required to access the knowledge that the Tear of the Abyss held.

Through their ancestral songs, they guided the crew in the execution of this ritual. The melodies filled the air with a magical energy, creating a deep sense of unity between the adventurers and the sea creatures around them.

The connection between humans and magical guardians of the sea was strengthened, paving the way for the next step in the quest for ancient knowledge.

The ritual began with the Pearl of the Abyss guarded in her chest and the golden necklace given by the naiads into Sarah's hands. The crew immersed themselves in the melodies of the mermaids and the words of the merfolk, creating a magical environment in the cavern. The guardians of the depths watched with deep respect.

As the ritual progressed, the Tear of the Abyss began to glow with dazzling light. The surrounding waters were filled with magical currents, and the crew experienced a connection not only with each other, but also with the sea itself.

It was evident that they were about to unveil the secrets they had so eagerly sought. Each member of the team could feel the magic of the sea flowing around them, preparing to reveal their ancient wisdom and knowledge.

At long last, the ritual reached its zenith, and the Tear of the Abyss emitted an extraordinary, brilliant light. A magical portal manifested at the very heart of the underwater cavern, unveiling a realm of profound knowledge and enigma that left the adventurers utterly astounded. This portal represented a gateway to an expanse of wisdom and secrets that they had never imagined.

The crew approached the portal, ready to access the knowledge contained in the Tear of the Abyss. Ethan, with his ability to comprehend ancient languages, went ahead and began to read the magical inscriptions surrounding the portal.

As he did so, the words came to life and formed images in everyone's minds.

The portal was like a window into the history of the North Sea, showing scenes of ancient civilizations, magical creatures, and important events that had shaped the region over the centuries.

Each crew member was fascinated by the vision unfolding before them, and they knew they were about to learn much more about the sea and their role in it.

Knowledge flowed to them, slowly unraveling the mysteries of the North Sea and its impact on the world. They learned about the ancient civilizations that had thrived in the region, building magical cities and establishing flourishing trade. They met the magical creatures that had been guardians of the sea for centuries, from the naiads that guarded coral reefs to the merfolk that kept the peace in the depths.

They also discovered the importance of maintaining balance in the sea, how even the slightest imbalance could trigger catastrophic consequences for the entire region and its inhabitants.

The knowledge that flowed from the Tear of the Abyss was filled with amazing stories and valuable lessons about the relationship between humanity and the mysterious North Sea.

The crew prepared to return to the surface, taking with them the knowledge and magic of the North Sea. United by their oath of allegiance and their bravery.

CHAPTER 10
THE RIDDLE OF THE CORAL MIRROR

As they prepared to continue their journey, exploring the cavern where they had activated the Tear of the Abyss, Liam noticed something that caught his attention. In one corner, among the rocks, was an unusual object: a coral mirror. This mirror had edges decorated with intricate marine designs and seemed to radiate a soft glow, as if it were alive.

Liam walked over to the coral mirror and picked it up carefully. To his surprise, it was surprisingly light and cool to the touch. As he held it in his hands, he began to notice something strange. On the surface of the mirror, images began to form, as if the mirror were a window to other times and places. The images seemed to dance in the mirror, showing scenes from faraway places and moments in the history of the North Sea. It was as if the coral mirror held secrets and additional knowledge that they were eager to reveal.

The crew gathered closely around Liam, their attention wholly captured by the captivating images that began to materialize on the reflective surface of the coral. These scenes seemed to flutter before their eyes, creating the sensation of witnessing both the historical past and events still to come simultaneously. The images unveiled significant moments in the rich history of the North Sea, as well as tantalizing glimpses of events that had not yet unfolded.

In one of the images, they saw ancient sailors in period costumes, exploring the depths of the sea in search of forgotten treasures. In another, they witnessed the creation

of the Tear of the Abyss by an ancient sorceress whose hands sparkled with magic. The images seemed to be connected in some

way to the secrets of the sea and the crew's search. Each scene unfolding in the coral mirror increased his curiosity and his desire to learn more about the mysterious North Sea. Ethan, whose deep comprehension of the mystical arts and sharp intuition were well-known among the crew, wasted no time in suggesting that the coral mirror held the key to unlocking the hidden wisdom of the North Sea. His idea revolved around the concept that this enigmatic object could

act as a bridge to unveil the profound knowledge concealed within the ocean's mysterious depths. As the crew gathered around, they listened with a mix of curiosity and anticipation, ready to explore the secrets of the sea as Ethan continued to explain his theory.

Perhaps, if they used it in the right way, they would be able to obtain clues that would lead them to the exact location of the Tear of the Abyss.

The crew embraced the idea and decided to experiment with the mysterious coral mirror. Sarah suggested one approach: that each crew member approach the mirror and focus on their desire to find the magic gem.

As they did so, the images in the mirror began to change, revealing clues and cues that could guide them in their search.

Each crew member hoped to uncover vital information to complete their mission and unravel the secrets of the North Sea.

Liam, intrigued and determined, took the initial step towards the mysterious coral mirror. With a sense of anticipation, he closed his eyes, delving deep into his thoughts, and concentrated on the mental image of the Tear of the Abyss. In his mind's eye, he envisioned the brilliant, radiant glow of the precious gem. It was as though his focused intent communicated with the mirror, initiating a reaction that sent ripples of mystical energy through the depths of the mirror's coral surface. The vision it displayed was nothing short of mesmerizing: a lighthouse perched on the shores of an unfamiliar island, its light cutting through the darkness of the night, illuminating the path to the unknown.

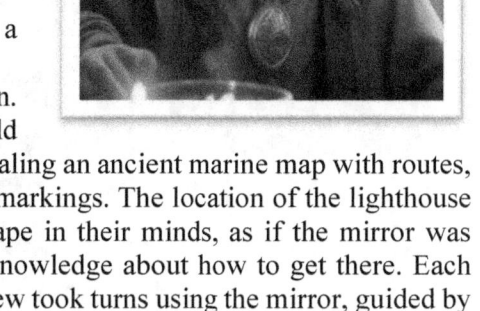

This beacon seemed to be the next step in their quest, a beacon that could bring them closer to their goal.

After Liam, Sarah approached the mirror with determination. He focused on the vision of the lighthouse and how they could get to it. The images in the mirror shifted and changed, revealing an ancient marine map with routes,

coordinates, and markings. The location of the lighthouse began to take shape in their minds, as if the mirror was sharing ancient knowledge about how to get there. Each member of the crew took turns using the mirror, guided by the hope that this magical item would give them the clues needed to move forward in their exciting quest.

Ethan, as a skilled master of magic, contributed his power to strengthen the connection with the enigmatic coral mirror. With his intervention, the images became sharper and more detailed, revealing even the specific features of the island and the lighthouse in question.

The mirror seemed to respond sensitively to their desires, guiding them precisely in their thrilling quest.

The crew continued to use the coral mirror, exploring different aspects of their search. They saw images of the challenges they still had to face, such as fierce storms and magical guardians guarding their path. In addition, they witnessed moments of triumph, such as the moment in which they would finally put their hands on the long-awaited Tear of the Abyss. Each vision provided by the mirror served as a constant reminder of their shared commitment and the magnitude of their adventure in the North Sea.

With each vision in the coral mirror, the crew felt more confident and prepared for their next leg of the journey. They had obtained valuable clues about the location of the lighthouse and what awaited them in their search for the Tear of the Abyss.

After thoroughly utilizing the mystical properties of the coral mirror, the crew collectively took a step back, their expressions a blend of fulfillment and anticipation. They had come to grasp the significance of their discovery and the role the coral mirror would play on their ongoing journey through the North Sea. It was a pivotal tool, a bridge to the enigmatic depths of knowledge hidden within the sea. With each revelation it offered, they were reminded of their purpose, and the mirror's mystical allure became an inseparable part of their quest.

They carefully decided to keep the coral mirror in their treasure chest, knowing that it would be a constant source of guidance on their journey. With the lighthouse on the coast of the unknown island as their next destination, they prepared to set sail, excited and ready to face the challenges and mysteries that awaited them.

Each crew member felt more united than ever, ready to overcome obstacles and continue their quest on this thrilling journey across the North Sea.

As they walked away from the cavern, the coral mirror emitted a soft glow, as if it was satisfied that it had served its purpose.

The crew moved forward united by their desire to find the Tear of the Abyss and solve the secrets that had been hidden in the North Sea for so long.

CHAPTER 11
JOURNEY INTO THE DARK ABYSS

Sarah, the group's expert navigator, took a close look at the map on which they had seen the coordinates reflected by the coral mirror. Deftly, he pointed toward the rocky shoreline in the distance, indicating the spot where he thought they would find the entrance to the lighthouse. However, as they approached the coast, they realized that it would not be an easy task. The access to the lighthouse was surrounded by strong currents and sharp rocks that made navigation dangerous. The sea was rough, and the wind was blowing hard, challenging their skills as navigators. The crew knew that they would have to work together and use all their experience to overcome this new challenge in their search for the Tear of the Abyss.

Waves crashed violently against the rocks surrounding the island, presenting an intimidating challenge to dock safely on shore.

The crew was acutely conscious of the need for a meticulous and precise approach to this maneuver, understanding that their ship, the steadfast companion on their daring adventure, was a vital asset. Guided by the lighthouse's beacon, they proceeded with utmost care, placing their trust in Sarah's leadership and her wealth of experience. She took charge of navigation, assuming the pivotal role of ensuring their safe arrival ashore. Every member of the crew remained vigilant, ready to execute Sarah's commands with precision, fully aware of the challenge awaiting them as they continued their quest for the Tear of the Abyss.

With remarkable agility and expertise, they executed a series of maneuvers, successfully guiding their vessel into a small, secluded cove nestled amidst towering rocks. The crew disembarked from the ship, their spirits high and determination unwavering, as they prepared to embark on their exploration of the island.

Their primary objective was to locate the entrance to the lighthouse, a crucial destination inspired by the visions seen in the coral mirror. The crew was resolute and eager to unravel the mysteries that lay ahead on this new and enigmatic terrain.

However, what they found on the island was nothing like what they had imagined. Surprise awaited as they began their exploration in a place full of mysteries and unknown challenges.

The rocky shoreline was covered with seaweed and lichens that grew due to constant exposure to salt water. This made the ground slippery and dangerous to walk on. In addition, the waves continued to crash against the rocks with force, creating a salty mist that filled the air and gave the island a mysterious atmosphere. The wind blowing from the sea was cold and carried with it a sense of adventure and mystery as the crew moved towards their next challenge in this unfamiliar land.

While venturing along the shoreline, the crew couldn't help but observe that the island was blanketed by a thick, impenetrable carpet of foliage. The trees, gnarled and entangled, along with the profusion of maritime vegetation, presented a formidable and intricate terrain, adding to the complexities of their expedition.

They knew they needed to be alert and focused as they searched for the entrance to the lighthouse. After walking through a thick kelp forest that looked like a natural labyrinth, they spotted a structure in the distance. This structure rose majestically from the island, and its angular shape and great height clearly indicated that it was the base of the lighthouse.

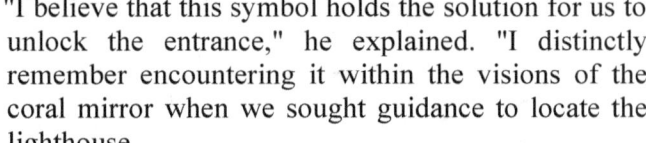

However, they noticed that access to the lighthouse was blocked by a solid iron gate. It was an obstacle they had to overcome in order to reach their goal.

The door looked very old and corroded by salt water and the passage of time.

It was evident that it functioned as a barrier to keep out unwanted intruders and protect the lighthouse. The crew gathered in front of the door, looking for a way to open it and gain access to the lighthouse. Liam took a close look at the door and noticed a strange inscription on the lock.

The inscription seemed to be a magical symbol, one he had seen in the coral mirror. He recalled the visions they had been shown how to open the lighthouse door and shared his discovery with the team. That inscription was the key they needed to move forward in their search.

Liam spoke with unwavering determination, "I believe that this symbol holds the solution for us to unlock the entrance," he explained. "I distinctly remember encountering it within the visions of the coral mirror when we sought guidance to locate the lighthouse.

It seems apparent that we must find a way to activate this symbol in order to gain access to whatever lies inside."

Ethan, with his deep knowledge of magic, approached the lock and began to examine the magic symbol carefully. He realized that he had to find a way to activate it to open the door. After a moment of concentration, he began to channel his magic into the lock, trying to figure out how to make the symbol light up and allow access to the lighthouse.

Ethan concentrated his magical abilities, allowing a radiant, golden thread of energy to extend toward the

36

intricate symbol. As his magic connected with the symbol, they felt a subtle vibration in the air, and the mechanism of the lock activated with a gentle, melodious hum. The door began to swing open, revealing the hidden passage beyond. The magic symbol shone brightly, and the iron gate slowly opened, revealing the entrance to the lighthouse. The crew proceeded cautiously, knowing that they were entering a place full of mystery and danger.

The interior of the lighthouse was in semi-darkness, with the only source of light coming from the lighthouse lantern at the top. The crew ascended a spiral staircase that led them to the top, where they hoped to find clues to the location of the Tear of the Abyss. Every step they took echoed off the stone staircase, creating an echo that filled the space. The darkness inside surrounded them, and the atmosphere seemed laden with secrets and whispers of the past. They knew they were about to face new challenges and needed to stay alert as they scouted the lighthouse for clues.

However, as they ascended, they realized that they were not alone in the lighthouse.

A menacing murmur began to echo through the air, and it felt as if dark secrets were lurking around every corner. Nightmarish creatures, the stuff of their worst dreams, emerged before them. These beings possessed razor-sharp claws and eyes that gleamed with malevolence, shrouded in shadows. They were the guardians of the lighthouse, ancient entities tasked with safeguarding its enigmatic mysteries. The crew realized that confronting these unforeseen challenges was essential as they pressed forward in their quest to reach the Tear of the Abyss at the pinnacle of the lighthouse.

The sea monsters, adorned with sharp claws that could shred steel and menacing fangs gleaming with malice, inched closer to the crew. With courage and determination, they steeled themselves to confront these formidable adversaries, recognizing that overcoming these creatures was a necessary step to continue their journey. The battle that unfolded at the lighthouse proved to be an intense and demanding trial.

The creatures launched their attacks fiercely, trying to impede the crew's advance. However, the crew stuck together and fought bravely. Each member of the team used their magical skills and powers to repel the sea monsters. The lighthouse lantern flickered with an intense light, casting flashes in the fight.

 The crew's determination was as fierce as that of the creatures that stood in their way. As the battle reached its climax, the sea monsters retreated and retreated into the shadows. The crew had been victorious, but they knew that their journey had not

yet come to an end. The top of the lighthouse remained an enigma, and the Tear of the Abyss waited, ready to reveal its secrets.

The fierce claws and menacing fangs of the sea monsters clashed with the crew's weapons and potent magic.

The ensuing combat was a grueling and rigorous test of their combat skills, strength, and stamina.

It was a harrowing struggle where every member of the crew had to push their limits to prevail.

The sea monsters were formidable, but the crew wasn't about to give up. The bravery and determination they had shown throughout their journey remained strong in this battle. Each member of the team used their skills and knowledge gained in their quest to bravely face the monsters. The crew knew they needed to stick together and fight as a team to overcome these terrifying adversaries. Despite the ferocity of the battle, they did not give ground, and slowly began to gain the upper hand against the sea monsters. The lighthouse lantern continued to shed its bright light, illuminating the fight amidst the darkness of the lighthouse.

With unwavering determination, the crew stood their ground, knowing that their safety and the pursuit of the Tear of the Abyss depended on their courage.

As the intense battle reached its peak, the sea monsters, unable to withstand the crew's tenacity, slowly slinked back into the darkness from which they had emerged. Victorious once more, the crew showcased their unwavering bravery and unyielding spirit in the face of formidable challenges.

They knew there were still challenges ahead, but they were ready to take on whatever it took to reach their goal.

Finally, after a grueling struggle, the crew managed to defeat the nightmarish creatures blocking their path. With courage and determination, they advanced to the top of the lighthouse, knowing that their goal was near. When they reached the top, they came

across a door that would lead them to the lighthouse lantern.

This was the high point of their search, the place where they hoped to find the long-awaited Tear of the Abyss. The door represented a final barrier they had to overcome in order to unravel the mysteries they had been pursuing.

The crew was ready to face any challenge this door might present, relying on the skills and drive they had demonstrated throughout their journey. They knew they were close to reaching their goal, and the suspense grew as they prepared to open the door and discover what awaited them in the lighthouse lantern.

The lantern of the lighthouse gave off a shimmering light that filled the room, creating a magical and wonderful atmosphere. In the center of the room, on a pedestal decorated with magical symbols, stood the Tear of the Abyss, a gem that radiated a magical and powerful glow. They had reached the heart of their quest, their ultimate goal. The Tear of the Abyss seemed to have an aura of wisdom and mystery that drew the crew to it.

After so many challenges and adventures, they finally had it at their fingertips, and they knew that they would soon discover the secrets and knowledge they craved so much.

However, the Tear of the Abyss was guarded by one last challenge. A magical riddle that they had to solve in order to access their wisdom. The crew gathered around the magic gem, ready to face this last hurdle in their quest.

The brilliance of the Tear of the Abyss, a priceless gem brimming with magical power, intensified and filled the room with its radiant glow. On the room's floor, an array of enchanting markings and

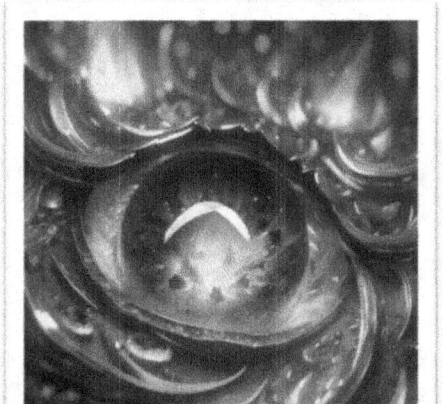

symbols illuminated with cryptic flashes, hinting at the mysteries they held. The crew recognized that the time had come to confront the enigma safeguarded by this precious magical gem. They stood prepared to uncover the secrets and knowledge concealed within the Tear of the Abyss, ready to embrace the revelations it would offer in this pivotal moment.

Collaborating as a tightly-knit team, the courageous crew harnessed their collective expertise and abilities to delve into the enigmatic magical puzzle encircling the Tear of the Abyss.

Gradually, they decoded its concealed secrets and unleashed the latent power contained within the magical gem. With each revelation, the riddle unfolded before their eyes, causing the Tear of the Abyss to gleam with an even more dazzling brilliance. The room was bathed in a mysterious, radiant light, offering a glimpse into the depths of its secrets.

They knew they were about to unveil ancient knowledge and occult powers that had been protected for a long time.

The wisdom emanating from the Tear of the Abyss flowed into the crew's minds like a river of knowledge. In the blink of an eye, they found themselves immersed in visions that showed them the past and future history of the North Sea. Through these visions, secrets that had remained hidden for centuries were revealed to them. The magical gem acted as a guide, revealing to them the purpose of their quest and the purpose of the quest.

Each crew member realized how important their role was in protecting and balancing the North Sea. They had been chosen for this mission and were committed to its success. The realization of their task filled them with determination and a sense of responsibility.

Emerging from the lighthouse, carrying the Tear of the Abyss, the crew felt satisfied and refreshed. Despite the challenges that still awaited them in the future, they were full of courage and determination to continue their search. They knew their journey had not come to an end and were prepared to face whatever fate had in store for them.

CHAPTER 12
MALACHOR'S MENACE

He continued his journey across the North Sea, carrying with him the Tear of the Abyss, the magical gem that had been the target of his quest. They knew they had to protect it at all costs, as this gem was vital to the North Sea and its secrets.

As they made their way to their next destination, a sense of unease filled the air. Liam, Sarah, Ethan, and the rest of the crew knew they were not alone in their search for the Tear of the Abyss. Malachor, the dark warlock who had chased the magic gem from the beginning, was still after them.

Malachor was a threat they could not underestimate. He had demonstrated his power in his attempt to obtain the Tear of the Abyss, and they were sure that he would not give up easily. The crew remained alert, aware that Malachor could appear at any moment.

The crew's journey was fraught with an underlying unease, knowing that a potential confrontation with the malevolent sorcerer, Malachor, loomed ahead. This looming threat cast a shadow over their adventure, intensifying the sense of apprehension. They were acutely aware that they had to remain vigilant and be fully ready to shield the precious magic gem, while also being prepared to confront any formidable challenges that Malachor might throw their way. The uncertain timing and location of their inevitable encounter with this adversary kept them in a constant state of readiness and anticipation as they pressed forward in their quest for answers and the safeguarding of the North Sea's well-being.

The chilling breeze swept across the ship's open deck, and the relentless waves pounded against the sturdy hull, creating a continuous, thunderous symphony of the sea. This atmospheric backdrop served as an ever-present reminder of the North Sea's unyielding power and the perils that lay in wait along their voyage.

The crew's unity and preparedness were paramount, a steadfast acknowledgment of the imperative need to stand as one and confront whatever trials the journey would throw their way. As they sailed, Sarah stared at the horizon for signs of Malachor. Her keen eyesight and experience as a navigator made her a watchful guardian.

Malachor's threat was real, and they were determined to protect the Tear of the Abyss from any attempted robbery.

The vast expanse of the sea lay before them, its endless blue horizon seeming to stretch out in every direction as far as the eye could see. A gentle breeze filled the sails as the ship forged ahead, carrying with it a sense of both anticipation and uncertainty. Sarah, with unwavering vigilance, diligently split her attention between the expansive sky above and the deep waters below.

Her keen eyes scanned each breaking wave for even the slightest hint of the dark warlock's looming presence. She studied every cloud that passed, searching for any ominous shapes or telltale signs that might reveal Malachor's whereabouts. It was a constant and painstaking watch to ensure their safety as they sailed deeper into the North Sea.

The crew relied on Sarah's skills to keep them safe from potential ambushes. They knew that the safety of the Tear of the Abyss depended on its ability to detect any threat. As they sailed the vast sea in their search for answers, they were prepared to meet any challenge that came their way.

The crew kept busy, preparing for what might come. Liam and Ethan discussed strategies to protect the magic gem and keep it out of Malachor's reach.

They knew they would face challenges on their journey, but they were willing to fight to protect what was theirs.

While traversing the open expanse of the sea, Liam and Ethan found themselves on the ship's deck, bathed in the warm and shimmering glow of the sun's reflection upon the water. In this serene setting, they engaged in hushed conversations, their heads close together as they exchanged thoughts and concerns about safeguarding the Tear of the Abyss. Both were well aware of the cunning and perilous nature of their adversary, Malachor, and the necessity of staying ahead of his schemes.

Their discussions led to several strategic decisions. First, they recognized the importance of maintaining a constant watch over the precious magical gem, even during the dark hours of night. To achieve this, they planned shifts among the crew, ensuring that there would always be a vigilant guardian in close proximity to the gem. This continuous vigilance would be their first line of defense.

Additionally, the two leaders of the group crafted a contingency plan for the potential encounter with Malachor. This strategy included detailed discussions of combat tactics, leveraging their knowledge of magic for protection, and how to respond swiftly to any unexpected threat. The aim was not just to protect the Tear of the Abyss, but also to outmaneuver their cunning enemy and secure the safety of the North Sea.

The crew was committed to protecting the Tear of the Abyss and knew that teamwork and preparedness was essential.

As they continued their journey, they clung to the determination to face any challenge the dark warlock might present in their quest for the magical gem.

Days passed as they made their way into the North Sea, nearing their next destination. The tension was palpable, and every member of the crew was alert, aware that their confrontation with Malachor was inevitable.

As night descended upon the vast sea, the crew's watchful eyes caught sight of a distant island on the horizon. This island, the very one they had glimpsed in the visions of the coral mirror, marked the next stage of their journey. Their hearts were filled with anticipation, knowing they were drawing near to their intended destination. Yet, they were all too aware of the perils that this enigmatic island held.

The island sat resolute amidst the churning waters, encircled by turbulent waves and towering cliffs that seemed to guard its mysterious secrets. The pale glow of the moon cast an eerie light on the rugged landscape, revealing shadows that danced mysteriously along the shoreline. As their ship drew nearer, the sailors couldn't shake an unsettling feeling that clung to the night air, as if the island concealed a tapestry of hidden enigmas and lurking dangers waiting to be uncovered.

Sarah, with her experience as a navigator, kept a close eye on ocean currents and the hidden dangers that could lurk beneath the surface of the water. She knew that docking on the island would be a challenge in itself, and they had to be cautious to avoid damaging his ship in the treacherous waters.

The crew was eager to explore the island and find out what awaited them, but they were also prepared to face any challenges that might arise. With the Tear of the Abyss in their possession and their unwavering determination, they were ready to face whatever fate had in store for them on this mysterious island.

As they approached the island, a dark shadow appeared on the horizon. A tall, hooded figure, with burning eyes, materialized in front of them. It was Malachor, the dark warlock who had pursued the Tear of the Abyss from the beginning.

Malachor's sinister laughter reverberated through the air as he steadily closed the distance between himself and the crew's ship. His malevolent intent was unmistakable; he was determined to seize the Tear of the Abyss, and he was ready to employ any means necessary to achieve his malevolent goals.

In response, the crew steeled themselves for the impending confrontation with the dark warlock. They fully understood the gravity of this moment; it was to be an epic battle that would not only challenge their courage but also push their skills to their limits. They

were resolute in their determination to protect the precious gem and thwart Malachor's wicked schemes.

With their weapons and magic at the ready, the crew lined up on the ship, ready to defend their treasure and face the mighty Malachor. The wind was blowing hard, flapping the ship's sails, as they neared a showdown with the dark warlock on the mysterious island.

The Tear of the Abyss shone brightly, as if aware of the coming struggle and ready to deploy its power in defense of those who guarded it.

Liam stepped forward, bravely, and headed for Malachor. "We will not allow you to seize the Tear of the Abyss.

We are ready to fight to protect it and preserve the balance of the North Sea."

Malachor, the malevolent sorcerer, retorted with a sinister and chilling laughter that sent shivers down the spines of the crew. "Very well, let the battle commence," he taunted. "But remember, courageous adventurers, my power is boundless, and your efforts will be futile unless you willingly surrender the magical gem."

The crew knew they were up against a formidable foe. Malachor's words only reinforced the gravity of the impending conflict, and they realized that defeating him would be an immense challenge.

Nevertheless, their determination remained unwavering, and they were committed to protecting the magic gem at all costs.

The tension in the air was palpable as both sides prepared for the showdown. They knew they were about to embark on a struggle of will and magic that would decide the fate of the Tear of the Abyss and the North Sea. The crew was united in their determination not to give in to Malachor's threats, no matter how powerful the dark warlock was.

The battle on the ship's deck was fierce. Malachor unleashed his dark magic, creating storms and shadows that engulfed the crew.

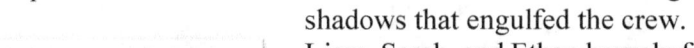
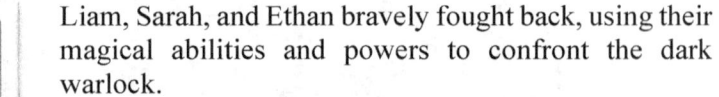

Liam, Sarah, and Ethan bravely fought back, using their magical abilities and powers to confront the dark warlock.

The battle raged on with great intensity and presented formidable challenges. The ship's deck transformed into a tumultuous battlefield where dazzling magical lights clashed with ominous shadows in a fierce contest of powers.

In the midst of the furious confrontation, Malachor, with a malevolent glint in his eyes, harnessed his dark powers to unleash searing bolts of lightning that streaked across the sky, illuminating the night with ominous brilliance. These bolts were like fiery serpents, hissing and crackling as they lashed out, threatening to engulf everything in their path.

44

In response, Liam, Sarah, and Ethan, fueled by their determination to protect the Tear of the Abyss, wielded their own formidable magical abilities. Brilliant flashes of radiant light erupted from their hands, casting a radiant, almost blinding glow. These bursts of magic were like celestial fireworks, illuminating the battlefield and dispelling the shadows that Malachor sought to use to his advantage. The wood of the ship, once steady and reliable beneath their feet, quivered under the relentless onslaught of magic, as if it too could feel the power of the conflict that raged above its planks.

Meanwhile, the sea, once calm and tranquil, now churned and thrashed in turmoil, echoing the fierce battle between the opposing magical forces. Waves rose and fell, mirroring the ebb and flow of the intense struggle that would determine the fate of the Tear of the Abyss.

As the clash continued, each member of the crew fought with unwavering determination, knowing that their mission to protect the Tear of the Abyss hinged on their ability to stand against the malevolent sorcerer. Their combined strength and unity became their greatest assets in the battle against Malachor.

Each crew member fought bravely, knowing that they were protecting something of great importance. The Tear of the Abyss shone brightly in the midst of the battle, as if channeling its power in support of the crew. They were determined not to allow Malachor to seize the magical gem and to preserve the balance of the North Sea at all costs.

Finally, after an epic battle that seemed to last forever, the crew managed to defeat Malachor. The dark sorcerer was ejected from the ship and disappeared into the sea, vowing vengeance.

They knew that Malachor would not give up easily, but they had proven their worth once again by protecting the Tear of the Abyss.

After the battle, the crew gathered on the deck of the ship, exhausted but triumphant. The Tear of the Abyss shone with an intense light in her hands, as if grateful for her bravery. They knew they had to continue their journey and that Malachor would continue to pursue them, but they were ready to face any challenge that stood in their way. They had become guardians of the North Sea and were willing to protect it at all costs.

CHAPTER 13
SHOWDOWN IN THE ANCIENT RUINS

The island loomed before them, with an ancient and mysterious atmosphere enveloping its shores. Dense vegetation covered most of the island, making it difficult for them to see what was inside. As they neared land, the crew knew they needed to be alert and prepared for any challenge that came their way.

The ancient ruins were an enigma unto themselves. No one knew who had built them or what their original purpose was. However, the legends spoke of the Tear of the Abyss, and the clues had led them here.

The ruins stood majestically in front of the crew, with ancient architecture and mysterious engravings on the stones. As they explored the site, they realized that the ruins were covered in ancient symbols and writings. Each step they took brought them one step closer to the mystery of the Tear of the Abyss and its role in the history of the North Sea.

The crew proceeded cautiously through the dense vegetation, with Sarah in the lead, looking for signs of the ruins. Each step took them deeper into the island, and they could feel the antiquity and mystery in the air. Finally, they came to a clearing in the forest, and in front of them stood the ancient ruins.

The ruins, a silent testament to a bygone era, rose majestically before the crew. Their sturdy stone walls, now adorned with the verdant embrace of moss and twisting vines, bore the weight of centuries of history. The engravings etched into the ancient stones appeared to hold within them the echoes of long-forgotten tales from ancient times, narrating stories and secrets that time had buried.

Amidst the crumbled stone and weathered inscriptions, the crew found themselves face to face with a puzzle from the past. These inscriptions, like cryptic whispers from history, revealed a language that had long faded into obscurity.

Their meaning remained elusive, challenging the crew's intellect and determination.

Yet, they held firm in their resolve, knowing that among these enigmatic symbols and inscriptions, they would unearth the key to unravel the mysteries of the Tear of the Abyss. With every careful examination of these ancient runes, they inched closer to their goal, ready to decipher the clues that would lead them on their quest for the truth.

The ruins were majestic and ancient, with stone columns reaching into the sky and decorative arches carved with magical symbols. The crew was amazed by the magnitude of the construction and the feeling that they were in a sacred place.

The stone columns were covered in vines and moss, as if nature herself had tried to reclaim these ancient structures. The magical symbols that adorned the arches emitted a soft glow, filling the place with a mystical aura.

It was evident that these ruins held deep and ancient secrets, and the crew was eager to explore and discover more about the Tear of the Abyss.

However, they had no time to waste. They knew that Malachor was following close behind, and they had to find the Tear of the Abyss before he did. They delved into the ruins, knowing they would face deadly traps and challenges on their way.

As they made their way through the ruins, they noticed magical inscriptions on the walls, which seemed to give clues as to the location of the Tear of the Abyss. Ethan, with his knowledge of magic, studied the inscriptions and tried to decipher their meaning.

"These inscriptions seem to be some kind of magic map," Ethan said. "They are leading us into the Tear of the Abyss, but they also warn of pitfalls and challenges on our path. We must be alert and follow the path carefully."

The inscriptions, etched in a long-forgotten magical script, began to disclose secrets of the ruins' inner workings. These cryptic messages held the key to navigating through the treacherous maze of the ancient structure while avoiding perilous traps and potential hazards. Each carefully crafted rune offered vital information, pointing the way forward and illuminating the intricate network of magic symbols that needed to be activated to unlock the path.

As the crew painstakingly deciphered these mystical engravings, a sense of anticipation filled the air. It was evident that the quest they embarked upon was not merely a physical journey but a test of their wits, resourcefulness, and mastery of the magical arts. The crew understood that every challenge they faced within these ancient ruins was an opportunity to prove their skill and cunning, forging their path forward through the tantalizing mysteries that lay ahead.

The crew followed the magical inscriptions, advancing through dark corridors and ruined

rooms. Magic traps were activated in their path, but they managed to get around them with skill. Each challenge they faced brought them closer to their goal.

After a journey filled with deciphering magical inscriptions and navigating through the winding maze of the ancient ruins, they reached a central chamber. In the heart of this room, atop an ornate stone pedestal, stood the Tear of the Abyss, radiating a brilliant and potent light, its power palpable and mesmerizing. The crew had finally arrived at their long-sought destination, and it was a moment of triumph. However, the weight of their achievement was accompanied by an unsettling realization – they were not the sole occupants of this hallowed chamber.

Out of the shadows emerged Malachor, he had followed the crew closely and was determined to obtain the Tear of the Abyss at any cost.

His tall, hooded figure stood at the entrance to the chamber, his eyes burning with a thirst for power. The crew prepared to face Malachor again, knowing that this would be the final battle for the Tear of the Abyss. Liam, Sarah, and Ethan stood their ground, ready to protect the magical gem from the dark warlock's clutches.

Liam, Sarah, and Ethan stood in front of the magical gem, determined to protect it. They knew that this would be their last battle against Malachor, and they were willing to fight to the end.

Malachor smiled wickedly as he prepared to unleash his dark magic. "This time, they won't run away from me. The Tear of the Abyss will be mine."

The ruin chamber was filled with palpable tension as the three crew members prepared to confront the dark warlock. The magic gem shone brightly on the pedestal, as if ready for a final act of resistance against Malachor's power.

The battle was about to begin, and magical lights and shadows collided in an epic showdown.

The battle that was fought in the ancient ruins was epic. Malachor unleashed his dark magic with fury, creating storms and shadows that engulfed the crew. Liam, Sarah, and Ethan fought bravely, using their magical skills and powers to confront the dark warlock.

The scene within the chamber was nothing short of spectacular, as the magical forces of the crew and Malachor entwined in a fierce battle. Brilliant beams of magical energy crisscrossed the air, creating an intricate dance of light and shadow that bathed the ancient ruins in a radiant display of clashing forces. The very air seemed to hum with the power of spells and incantations as the crew, consisting of

Liam, Sarah, and Ethan, pushed themselves to their limits in an unyielding struggle against the dark sorcerer, Malachor.

The camera echoed with rumblings and magical thunder as the battle intensified. Each of the combatants was determined to protect the Tear of the Abyss and ensure that it did not fall into the hands of the dark warlock.

The ruins resounded with the clash of magical powers, and the inscriptions on the walls seemed to come to life. The fighting was intense and challenging, but the crew did not give up.

Finally, after a battle that seemed to last forever, the crew managed to defeat Malachor. The dark warlock was expelled from the ruins and disappeared into the shadows, vowing vengeance.

The crew gathered in the ruin chamber, exhausted but victorious. The Tear of the Abyss was safe in his possession.

CHAPTER 14
SUPERNATURAL ABILITIES

After the intense battle with Malachor, Liam's team was exhausted but overjoyed. The Tear of the Abyss, which had been the center of the struggle, now shone with dazzling intensity. It was as if the confrontation with the dark sorcerer had strengthened his power. As the gem gave off its brilliant glow, a magical energy flowed around it, like an invisible river of supernatural knowledge and abilities.

Liam's team was completely captivated by the dazzling glow of the Tear of the Abyss. The gem radiated a soft light and emitted a magical hum, as if it was trying to communicate with them in a special language that only they could understand. They approached cautiously, feeling how that magical energy flowed around them, enveloping them like a powerful magnet that irresistibly drew them towards the glittering gem.

It was as if they were being called by a greater force that led them to the knowledge and power that awaited them.

The magic was palpable in the air, and the curiosity and excitement of the team members grew as they moved towards this source of mystery and change in their lives.

Ethan, whose eyes shone with an intense desire to know, was the first to reach out to the gem. When his fingers touched the surface of the Tear of the Abyss, he experienced a surge of knowledge flowing straight into his mind. He closed his eyes and focused, allowing the flood of wisdom to flood in. At that moment, the world became transparent to him.

He realized that he could feel the energy of everything around him. This means that he could feel the force emanating from every object and every living creature that was near him. There were no more hidden secrets for him. He could feel even the tiny dust particles floating in the air, and he could also understand people's deepest thoughts and emotions.

Imagine that he had a kind of sixth sense that allowed him to perceive everything around him.

Also, he was able to see how things worked. Not only did I understand what they were, but I knew why they existed and how they were connected to each other. This gave him a deep understanding of the world. It was as if he had opened a giant book containing all the secrets and knowledge of the world, and he could read it at will. It was an

incredible power that made him feel like he had the entire universe at his disposal, and he was willing to use it for the good of all.

Liam, after seeing how brave Ethan was in touching the Tear of the Abyss, was inspired and reached out to the gem. When his fingers touched the surface of the Teardrop, something extraordinary happened: it was as if a wave of magic enveloped him completely.

Suddenly, his body became light, as if the force of gravity no longer had control over him. It was as if he could float in the air.

Most astonishing of all, just thinking about it, Liam lifted his feet off the ground and rose a few inches above the ground. It was a truly incredible experience, both for him and for his peers who watched in awe. Imagine that

you suddenly have the ability to fly, like a bird in the sky. The force that normally keeps you glued to the ground is no longer an obstacle.

Liam experienced a sense of lightness and freedom that he had never felt before. It was as if gravity no longer had power over him, as if he could defy the laws of physics. His friends watched as he

rose before their eyes, and their faces reflected surprise and admiration.

It was a magical moment when the possibility of flying had become real.

Liam knew that this new ability would change his life in amazing ways. He realized that he now had a unique advantage, a skill that would allow him to explore the world from a completely different perspective. The earth was no longer a limit, and the sky was at his fingertips. He was excited by all the possibilities that opened up before him and was determined to make the most of this new skill. In addition, he knew that with this power also came great responsibility, and he was ready to use it to protect his team and face the challenges that lay ahead. It was an amazing moment in their lives that would change their destiny forever.

Sarah, unable to resist the temptation to discover the wonders that the Tear of the Abyss offered, gently reached out to the gem.

The very instant her fingers made contact with the surface of the Teardrop, something amazing happened. Her mind was filled with soft, peaceful whispers that seemed to flow straight from the depths of the sea. They were the voices of sea creatures, whispering their secrets and desires to her in a language only she could understand.

For Sarah, this gift was like becoming the protector and confidant of the waters of the North Sea. It was as if the ocean entrusted her with all its secrets and she became the guardian of its vast underwater kingdom.

This extraordinary gift granted him the ability to delve into the underwater world in a unique and profound way. Sarah could explore the mysteries and wonders of the deep ocean with a special connection. This new ability filled her with awe and gratitude, as she could now know and understand the underwater world in a way that no one else could.

Together, Liam, Ethan, and Sarah shared their newfound skills with the rest of the team. Their lives had changed in ways they could never have imagined. They were the guardians of ancient knowledge and unparalleled magical power. Not only had they gained these abilities in their own right, but they had acquired them through their bravery in battle against Malachor.

They looked at each other, understanding the magnitude of what had been bestowed upon them. They decided to use their gifts to protect the North Sea and its secrets.

The glow of the abyss tear began to subside, but the skills they had acquired were still intact. Now they had to learn to control and master their powers.

CHAPTER 15
THE FINAL BATTLE

The crew had become guardians of the North Sea, with supernatural abilities bestowed by the Tear of the Abyss. They were willing to use their newfound powers to protect the sea and its secrets, but the threat of Malachor was still present, stalking them every step of the way.

Liam's beloved homeland, Eldoria, found itself in the throes of an imminent peril. The relentless and vengeful spirit of Malachor, undeterred by his prior defeat in their epic magical confrontation, continued to loom ominously, harboring an unquenchable thirst for retribution. His sinister ambition knew no bounds, and he remained steadfastly determined to wrest the Tear of the Abyss from its guardians. He was acutely aware of the unparalleled potency encapsulated within this mystical gem, recognizing it as the ultimate key to safeguarding the North Sea and the profound enigmas concealed beneath its depths.

Yet, Malachor's malevolent intentions knew no limits, as he hankered to harness this very power to further his nefarious and dark objectives, relentlessly posing a grave and looming threat to the hallowed secrets of the North Sea.

As they sailed toward Eldoria. They knew that a final battle with Malachor was imminent, and they were willing to fight for the fate of their homeland.

Liam knew he had to protect his home and his people from the threat of Malachor. With his newfound supernatural powers, he felt more prepared than ever to face the dark warlock.

The crew's unity was unbreakable, a testament to their unwavering commitment to protect their cherished homeland, Eldoria, and the mystical North Sea from the sinister machinations of Malachor.

Among their ranks, Emma utilized her remarkable telepathic abilities to communicate with the sea's denizens, creating a vital connection that ensured their preparedness to rally to their aid if ever called upon.

In the meantime, Ethan, the adept in the mystic arts, meticulously readied an impressive array of potent spells, a reflection of his determination to confront Malachor and wield his newfound powers to their fullest extent. It was in these moments of collaboration and preparation that their collective strength truly shone, as they geared up for the inevitable and momentous confrontation ahead.

Finally, they reached the shores of Eldoria, and found Malachor waiting for them. The dark warlock was willing to do anything to obtain the Tear of the Abyss, and had gathered an army of dark magical creatures to confront the crew.

The final battle began with an explosion of magic and fury.

Liam, Sarah, Ethan, and Emma, the dedicated team exhibited unwavering bravery and determination as they fearlessly plunged into a grueling and harrowing battle. Drawing upon the newfound supernatural powers they had gained, they faced off against a legion of fearsome magical creatures.

The crew found themselves face to face with a troupe of truly nightmarish creatures. These vile beings were armed with the menacing features of razor-sharp fangs and deadly claws, which made them a truly formidable and perilous threat. It was a situation that could easily have filled the bravest hearts with dread. However, the crew's spirit remained resolute and undaunted in the presence of these ominous foes. Far from yielding to fear, they stood tall and steadfast, unwavering in their resolve to overcome this formidable challenge. Their indomitable courage propelled them to face this ordeal head-on, as they remained committed to the singular goal of emerging triumphant.

Each deployed their magical abilities learned during their journey, creating protective shields and launching magic beams. The bright lights of his magic mingled with the darkness of Malachor's creatures in a supernatural spectacle.

Emma, guided by his mastery of the arcane arts, deftly harnessed the very elements of the ocean with her magical prowess. She wove spells that shaped the turbulent seas into powerful whirlwinds and towering waves, acting as a mighty force that surged forth to cleanse their surroundings of the menacing minions under the command of Malachor. Her eyes took on a luminous, entrancing hue of profound azure, a telltale sign that she was deeply attuned to the magic coursing through her, and that she was fully immersed in the utilization of his extraordinary abilities.

The sea seemed to answer their call, forming waves and whirlpools that shielded the team from the terrifying creatures.

The combination of her determination and magical abilities made her a powerful force in battle.

With each gesture, she manipulated the waters of the sea to repel dark creatures that threatened to get too close.

Sarah bravely joined the battle mounted on a dolphin, and behind her, a group of friendly sea creatures who had decided to support her cause. Together, they created a tall and powerful wall of water that stood between the crew and the attacks of Malachor's dark creatures. The glare of the sun reflected off the water, making the wall of sparkling water look like a natural fortress. It was a demonstration of the alliance between the sea beings and the brave human adventurers in the fight

against the darkness. Sarah deftly led her group of aquatic allies, controlling the flow of the water with her magic and experience as a navigator.

The colossal wall of water, conjured by Liam's exceptional command over the ocean's elements, played a dual role on the battlefield. First and foremost, it acted as an indomitable defensive shield, intercepting the malevolent onslaught of attacks launched by the sinister entities under Malachor's dominion.

Secondly, it functioned as a protective fortress, sheltering the valiant crew members from the relentless assault of the nightmarish creatures aligned with the dark warlock.

This impressive defense wasn't the product of individual effort but rather the culmination of a remarkable collaboration between the crew and the sea creatures. Their unwavering unity, fueled by their shared mission and their devotion to safeguarding their homeland, solidified this awe-inspiring alliance, making the barrier nearly impervious to the forces of darkness.

Ethan unleashed his magic with great dexterity, casting spells of great power that disarmed and weakened Malachor's creatures.

Masrk´s mastery over the magical currents of the North Sea proved to be nothing short of remarkable. His exceptional skill in manipulating these mystical forces played a pivotal role in ensuring the safety of the crew during the harrowing and ferocious confrontation with the dark minions of Malachor.

Each incantation and spell he conjured resembled radiant beams of light piercing through the oppressive darkness of the battle, releasing powerful surges of energy that acted as a forceful reprieve. The creatures under Malachor's dominion were forcefully pushed back.

The crew, their expressions a mix of awe and gratitude, witnessed the incredible might of Ethan's abilities as they beheld the dark creatures of Malachor being effectively subdued by the relentless

power of his magic. This strategic advantage granted them a crucial respite, allowing them to maintain their safety and counter-attack with renewed determination.

Ethan's magic was a powerful force in this fight against the darkness, and his mastery over the magical currents of the sea had become an invaluable defense for the team.

The battle turned into an epic showdown that spanned all of Eldoria, with explosions of magic, lightning, and clashes of supernatural powers filling the air.

The crew members showed impressive bravery as they were determined to protect their beloved homeland and, of course, the precious Tear of the Abyss. The battle raged, and the explosions of magic were like magical fireworks that lit up the sky and made the earth tremble. The clashes of magical powers created waves of energy that spread throughout the region, shaking the foundations of Eldoria. The crew was undeterred by the scale of the battle and stood firm, determined to prevail in this fight to protect their world and their home.

Each member of the team was a force of nature in their own right, and together they formed an unstoppable squad determined to stand up for what was important to them.

Malachor, on the other hand, was not far behind and proved to be a formidable adversary. With a gesture and mysterious words, he unleashed dark spells that darkened the sky and covered the battlefield with a menacing shadow.

He was determined to obtain the Tear of the Abyss and use its power for his dark and self-centered ends. His every move was filled with magical malevolence, and his determination was evident in his fiery eyes. The confrontation between Malachor and the crew promised to be a showdown of epic proportions.

After an arduous and grueling battle that pushed their abilities and stamina to the limits, Liam, along with his determined team, achieved a hard-fought victory over Malachor.

Malachor was banished from the lands he had threatened, gradually receding into the darkness and obscurity, where his sinister intent could no longer harm their homeland.

This hard-fought battle served as a poignant testament to the unwavering determination and unyielding resilience of the crew, who had pledged to safeguard their beloved Eldoria and the North Sea from the clutches of evil.

The crew's victory was a testament to their bravery and determination to protect their homeland and the Tear of the Abyss.

Eldoria's fate was safe, and the Tear of the Abyss remained in her possession, ready to protect the sea and its secrets.

The crew had overcome unimaginable challenges in their mission to protect the North Sea and preserve its magic. Their journey had not been easy, but they had shown that they were willing to fight for what they believed in.

CHAPTER 16
THE RETURN TO ELDORIA

The return journey to Eldoria served as a time of reflection and contemplation for Liam and his team. In the climactic showdown against Malachor and his malevolent minions, they had not only showcased their unwavering courage but also unearthed the significance of camaraderie and selflessness. These invaluable lessons were forged in the crucible of adversity, uniting them in a bond stronger than ever.

Their mission was clear: to safeguard the North Sea and its ancient, enigmatic magic from potential threats. The intricate web of power and balance within the sea had to be maintained, and the age-old arcane secrets preserved for the generations to come. This journey had transformed them into not just protectors of their homeland but also stewards of a cherished legacy, bound by duty to uphold the sanctity of the sea's ancient magic.

During the return voyage to Eldoria, Sarah, Liam, Emma and Ethan convened on the ship's deck, their faces etched with expressions of contemplation and determination. It was a moment of shared reflection, as they weighed the profound significance of the Tear of the Abyss, a gem pulsating with formidable magic.

Liam's words carried the weight of responsibility and wisdom as he broached the subject. "The Tear of the Abyss is no ordinary gem; its magic is immensely powerful. It is our duty to use its powers judiciously and with great care. We must be the custodians of the North Sea's ancient secrets, recognizing the gravity of our mission."

Ethan, his eyes infused with the gleam of newfound knowledge, interjected, "Our

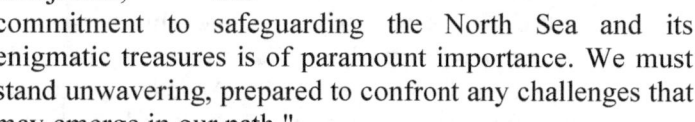

commitment to safeguarding the North Sea and its enigmatic treasures is of paramount importance. We must stand unwavering, prepared to confront any challenges that may emerge in our path."

During their earnest discussion, the friends engaged in a heartfelt exchange of ideas about how to ensure the safety of the Tear of the Abyss. They also contemplated ways to harness its formidable magical powers for the overarching goal of upholding equilibrium in the North Sea. With an unswerving resolve, they were dedicated to deepening their understanding of this mystical gem and unlocking its potential. This knowledge, they believed, was the key to their mission: safeguarding the cherished marine realm that they called home, preserving the ancient enchantments that had endured through generations.

They remained fully aware that the journey ahead would be fraught with challenges, but they were wholeheartedly committed to confronting any obstacle that arose.

Their mission was clear: to protect and nurture the sea they held so dear.

Emma´s solemn agreement came in the form of a nod, a gesture that encapsulated the unspoken understanding shared among the friends.

With a gentle but resolute tone, she underscored the profound significance of their bonds and the willingness to make sacrifices. "Our friendship and our unwavering readiness to put ourselves on the line were pivotal elements that secured our triumph over Malachor," she emphasized.

In a voice that resonated with determination, she continued, "It is incumbent upon us to etch our mission deeply into our hearts: the safeguarding of the sea and its irreplaceable magic." Emma´s words acted as a reminder of their collective purpose, serving as a compass guiding them through the uncharted waters of their continuing journey.

As they engaged in their profound conversation, Sarah accentuated the significance of their unity and the unwavering trust they had cultivated among themselves. This bond had served as an unshakable foundation that enabled them to confront and overcome the formidable challenges that had crossed their path.

She passionately stressed their role as guardians of the North Sea, underscoring the immense responsibility that rested upon their shoulders.

Sarah also called upon them to exercise courage and wisdom in their endeavors to protect and perpetuate the sea's enigmatic wonders and the enduring magic that had been cherished for generations.

They were acutely aware that their friendship and wholehearted commitment to their shared cause were their most potent assets as they steeled themselves to confront whatever trials lay ahead on the horizon.

Ethan, the revered authority in the realm of magic and its intricacies, seamlessly integrated his perspective into their ongoing conversation. With an air of profound wisdom, he expounded, "The Tear of the Abyss has graciously endowed us with extraordinary and unparalleled magical endowments. It is of paramount importance that we embark on a journey to fathom its very essence meticulously and comprehensively."

His words radiated with a sense of reverence for the magical artifact they now safeguarded, underscoring the need to unravel its hidden potential. This understanding, he believed, was the cornerstone of their journey to fulfill their mission with success.

In his reflection, Ethan emphasized the importance of fully understanding the magical powers they had gained through the Tear of the Abyss.

Ethan, possessing profound insight into their roles as protectors of the North Sea, recognized that their efficacy hinged upon their mastery and judicious application of the supernatural powers they had recently acquired. This, in turn, necessitated a dedicated and unwavering commitment to the relentless pursuit of magical knowledge and expertise. Additionally, they must cultivate a deep comprehension of how to wield these newfound abilities for the betterment of their overarching mission: the safeguarding and preservation of the sea and its enigmatic treasures.

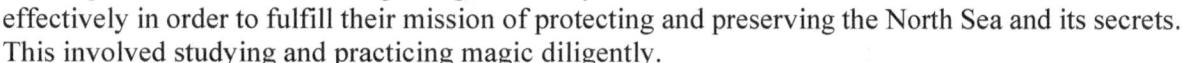

In simpler terms, Ethan stressed the importance of them learning how to use their magical gifts wisely and effectively in order to fulfill their mission of protecting and preserving the North Sea and its secrets. This involved studying and practicing magic diligently.

As they made their way to the familiar shores of Eldoria, the crew was immersed in preparations for their imminent victorious return. The thrilling news of his triumph over Malachor had already spread throughout Liam's homeland, and the populace awaited with great anticipation the return of the heroes who had protected his home.

In the coastal villages and towns of Eldoria, people gathered to welcome Liam, Sarah, Ethan, Emma and the rest of the crew. Flags flew in the streets, and the inhabitants dressed in their best attire in honor of their brave defenders.

The atmosphere was filled with joy and gratitude, and the excitement was palpable as they approached the shores they loved so much and had protected once again.

Upon their return, Eldoria warmly embraced their triumphant heroes, ushering in an atmosphere of unbridled joy and festivities. The crew was lauded and celebrated as genuine champions, and the overwhelming gratitude of the Eldorian populace towards them was unmistakable. Every individual in Liam's homeland, Sarah, Ethan, and the entire crew, held a profound and genuine appreciation for their unparalleled valor in safeguarding the North Sea.

In simpler terms, when they arrived back in Eldoria, the people welcomed them with open arms and celebrated them as heroes. The folks of Eldoria were incredibly thankful for their bravery in protecting the North Sea.

The Tear of the Abyss, which had demanded their bravery and courage, now stood as a powerful symbol of hope and security for the residents of Eldoria. This precious magical gem found a place of honor at the heart of the city, serving as a perpetual testament to the unwavering determination and valor exhibited by the crew.

The residents held a deep belief that, with the Tear of the Abyss under their protection, Eldoria would remain shielded from any forthcoming perils. This assurance infused the people with a sense of confidence and tranquility concerning the days to come.

To guarantee the security of the sea and effectively utilize the magical potential of the Tear of the Abyss, the crew resolved to create a permanent stronghold on Eldoria. This base would serve as the central command center for their operations in safeguarding the North Sea.

Establishing a base on Eldoria was a decision of great significance. This move positioned the crew at the heart of their operations, providing them with a central hub from which they could meticulously plan and coordinate their actions in response to sea-related challenges. This strategic location ensured that they could respond quickly and efficiently to emerging threats, safeguarding the North Sea and its secrets.

In addition to its strategic importance, the base offered a secure and controlled environment for their ongoing research into the Tear of the Abyss. This research was essential for unraveling the gem's potential and gaining a deeper understanding of its enigmatic powers. By doing so, they were not only enhancing their own capabilities but also strengthening their connection to the people of Eldoria and the broader marine protection mission.

This base served as a physical representation of their commitment to safeguarding the sea and its magical heritage. It was a testament to their determination to protect their home, and it would play a pivotal role in their ongoing efforts to preserve the North Sea's secrets for generations to come.

www.ingramcontent.com/pod-product-compliance
Lightning Source LLC
Chambersburg PA
CBHW080851120626
46546CB00008B/2788

9781963159073